EXPLORING

To Julie,
who shares my pack,
inspires my dreams,
and deeply loves
this Peninsula, named
Door

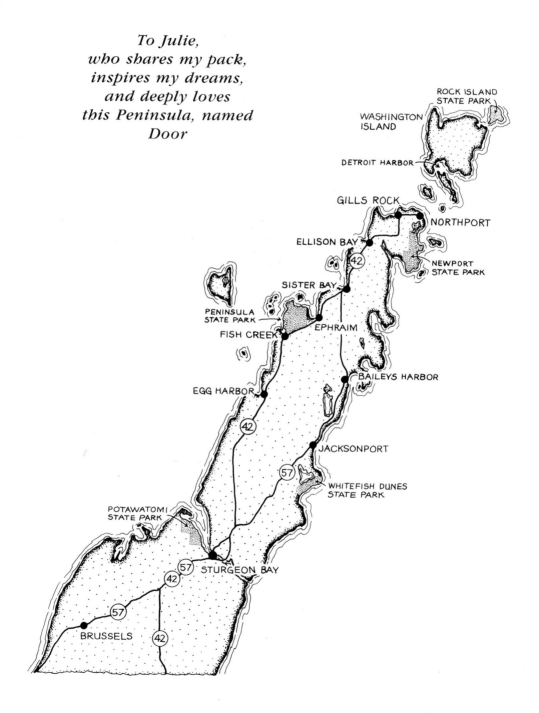

EXPLORING
Door County

Craig Charles

NorthWord
PRESS, INC.

FROM THE NORTHWORD
NATURE GUIDE COLLECTION

Published By:

NorthWord Press, Inc.
Box 1360
Minocqua, WI 54548

Designed by Moonlit Ink, Madison, Wisconsin

For a Free Catalog describing NorthWord's line of
nature books and gifts, call 1-800-336-5666

ISBN 1-55971-011-X

Printed in Singapore through Palace Press

PREFACE

Door County captured my interest at an early age. It lured me away from my Peninsula State Park campsite and hid me in a cedar forest, much to the dismay of park rangers searching for this lost seven-year-old. The peninsula hasn't lost its grip.

Today, the lakeshore waves that pound Door County crest beneath my sea kayak, and the peninsula's quaint country roads disappear beneath the tires of my 10-speed. Its forests still shelter my hiking boots from a world of rapid transit while its beautiful beaches provide a welcome pillow of sand on a lazy summer day.

This guide will take you off Door County's well-traveled paths into a world of secluded beaches, isolated campsites and deserted country roads. You'll be encouraged to stroll, backpack, pedal, ski and paddle to experience Door County at its natural best.

But the Door Peninsula is a fragile place—a delicate balance of rock, lake and land that demands special consideration and protection. Now, the responsibility for this constant vigilance is in your hands, because you've just begun *Exploring Door County*.

Symbol Key

swimming

boating

canoeing and kayaking

fishing

nature trails

hiking trails

biking trails

horeseback trails

cross country ski trails

snowmobile trails

overlook and vista

historical significance

camping

camping with electrical outlets

boat ramp

picnic area

handicapped picnic area and restrooms

area overview

cities, towns & villages

wildlife area, refuge, preserve

TABLE OF CONTENTS

INTRODUCTION

The Door Peninsula is a land of striking natural beauty, rich in ethnic heritage and cultural values. Door County leads all other Wisconsin counties with nearly 250 coastal miles on the surrounding waters of Lake Michigan and Green Bay. These waterways are part of a larger, more complex system that includes tributary lakes, streams and wetlands.

Door County's overwhelming natural beauty is due largely to the geology of the region. Carved by glacial action, the county is a spectacular limestone peninsula that juts 80 miles into Lake Michigan. Known as the Niagara Escarpment, this limestone ledge is recognizable to travelers heading north from Green Bay enjoying the magnificent bay shore view. The escarpment forms the rugged backbone of the entire Door Peninsula and arcs through Canada over 900 miles to New York State, where it supports the plunging waters of Niagara Falls.

The terrain on the peninsula is sometimes gentle and forgiving, often wild and rugged. Rocky limestone cliffs give way to sandy beaches on the western shore of the peninsula, while verdant forests meet marshy bays on the eastern shore. Over 30 caves are known to exist in Door County, including Tecumseh, the longest cave in Wisconsin, near the village of Egg Harbor.

Over 200 shipwrecks lie scattered along the Door Peninsula shoreline, providing an eerie grave for unfortunate mariners lost at sea. Many of those sailors met their demise in the treacherous passage at the tip of Door County known as Porte des Morts, or Death's Door. The county owes its name to this dangerous strait and even today modern visitors can still feel the danger felt by early sailors when at Gill's Rock, the waters of Green Bay meet the waters of Lake Michigan in a violent clash of surf and spray.

Today, ferries routinely shuttle both autos and passengers from the Door County mainland across Death's Door Strait to Washington Island in safety and comfort, but adventuresome sea kayakers still chal-

Oh, that glorious Wisconsin wilderness!
Everything new and pure . . . Young hearts, young leaves, flowers, animals, the winds and the streams and the sparkling lakes all rejoicing together.
—John Muir

(opposite page)

Wind and waves combine to carve rugged sea caves from Door County's rocky lakeshore.

1

lenge the passage as did the earliest mariners, with pack and paddle, keeping the legend alive.

Sandwiched by Green Bay to the west and Lake Michigan to the east, Door tops all other Wisconsin counties in parks and nature preserves. Adventurers will find over 100 miles of trails for hiking, biking and skiing. These maintained trails traverse five state parks, meander through nature preserves and skirt both rugged bluffs and sandy beaches.

The folks who live here are as varied as the terrain. The peninsula is an ethnic melting pot. Washington Island at the northern end of the county was settled by Icelanders, while the village of Brussels at the peninsula's southern end remains a stronghold of Belgian ancestry. A countywide census completed in the 1870s found settlers from Prussia, Bohemia, Ireland, Norway, Sweden, Denmark and Canada. Today bratwurst and beer are found at nearly every summer festival in the county, attesting to the strong German heritage that remains on this splendid peninsula.

The natural beauty of the area continues to draw artists, writers and craftspeople to its shores. Today these folks offer visitors a variety of cultural experiences, including dance, art, theater and literature, unsurpassed in America's heartland.

A 1914 publication of the United Fruit Growers Company touts Door County as the "California of the North." That may be stretching the truth a bit, but the fact of the matter is that the Door Peninsula does enjoy a climate somewhat better than its northern neighbors do. The village of Jacksonport lies on the 45th meridian, halfway between the North Pole and the Equator. Sandwiched by the waters of Lake Michigan to the east and Green Bay to the west, the peninsula is somewhat cushioned from winter's iciest blasts and summer's scorching heat waves. However, temperatures on the peninsula can vary dramatically and visitors should carry a wide range of clothing.

The influence of Lake Michigan becomes most evident on those occasions when an eight-mile trip from the bay side of the peninsula to the lakeshore means a ten-degree temperature drop in summer. During winter, lake effect snowstorms have been

2

known to drop ten inches of snow on the peninsula's lakeshore while the bay side receives only a dusting. This will come as good news to skiers since the lakeshore is blessed with some of the finest cross-country ski trails in mid-America.

Partly due to its climate, the Door Peninsula remains the third-largest cherry-producing area in the nation. It also produces 40% of Wisconsin's apple crop. May finds the fruit trees in bloom as an explosion of pink and white blossoms marks the beginning of the summer season. Mid- to late July is cherry-picking time and a great time to visit "cherryland."

You can get to Door County by air, land or water. Austin Straubel Field in Green Bay is served by Northwest Orient and United airlines. Cherryland Airport in Sturgeon Bay is served by Alliance Airlines with daily round-trip flights to Chicago. Rental cars are available in Green Bay and Sturgeon Bay.

The city of Green Bay, Wisconsin, lies at the western base of the Door Peninsula, and most visitors pass through this industrial workhorse en route to Door County. Extending east of this city lies Wisconsin State Highway 29. For practical and geographical reasons this highway forms the imaginary base of the Door Peninsula as it meets the Lake Michigan shore in the picturesque coastal community of Kewaunee.

Visitors to Door County typically arrive via Interstate 43 from Milwaukee and Chicago, Highway 29 from Minneapolis–St. Paul and Highway 41-141 from the north country. These highways converge in Green Bay, where travelers are funneled into Door County via two-lane Highway 57.

If you're lost, the Door County Chamber of Commerce will give you directions. Their phone is 414-743-4456.

You can cross Lake Michigan on a passenger and car ferry from Ludington, Michigan, to Kewaunee, Wisconsin. Daily service is offered year-round. For current schedule information, phone 800-253-0094.

Lodging facilities on the Door Peninsula range from rustic bay shore cottages to modern year-round motels complete with indoor pools, whirlpools and saunas. Prices are seasonal, reaching a peak during

MEET INCREASE CLAFLIN, PENINSULA PIONEER
Increase Claflin and his wife, Mary, became Door County's first permanent white settlers when they built a cabin at Little Sturgeon Bay in 1835. When other settlers broke Claflin's solitude, Increase moved up the Peninsula becoming the first permanent white settler at the village that still bears the name he chose, Fish Creek.

3

the summer months and over the New Year holiday. Prices also depend on which village, town or city you wish to visit. In general, Sturgeon Bay offers the most affordable accommodations while Ephraim offers the most exclusive and expensive.

Bed-and-breakfast inns are gaining in popularity. A few of these establishments offer not only turn-of-the-century atmosphere, but 21st century amenities as well, including in-room whirlpools and showers. Other bed-and-breakfast inns provide an opportunity to stay with the locals and get an insider's view of life on the peninsula.

Cottages remain the most popular and affordable lodging alternative for families. Many hotels and motels here do not allow children and pets, making cottages not only a pleasant alternative but a true necessity.

Since the early 1980s when visitors often found "no vacancy" signs on busy summer weekends, a hotel/motel/condominium construction boom has occurred. This has expanded both the number of beds and the variety of accommodations available. Some long-time visitors have complained about this construction boom, and developers are becoming sensitive to this criticism, building facilities that blend rather than clash with the landscape.

Despite increased lodging opportunities, reservations are still highly recommended to avoid disappointment. The best source for current information is the Door County Chamber of Commerce, 414-743-4456. Tell the chamber where you'd like to stay, your budget limitations and what type of accommodations you're looking for, and they'll give you several options. If you arrive at the chamber of commerce office in Sturgeon Bay without a reservation, you'll find a TRIPhone there to help you locate available accommodations.

Door County's five state parks harbor the priceless gems of the peninsula. Towering limestone cliffs meet clear blue waters at Peninsula State Park. Endangered plants anchor ancient sand dunes at Whitefish Dunes State Park. Cool Lake Michigan winds fan Rock Island State Park. Ruffed grouse explode from

THE COTTAGE LIFE

Most housekeeping units on the peninsula rent from Saturday to Saturday during the summer season. A few may rent for two- or three-night minimums, especially during fall, winter and spring..

the verdant forest of Newport State Park, and white-tail deer find shelter in the wooded hills of Pota-watomi State Park.

Much of the natural beauty of the peninsula has been preserved in these state parks, as well as in county and town parks and nature preserves. These parks contain delicate and complex ecosystems har-boring endangered plant communities. While the parks are designed for fun and relaxation, they re-quire responsible camping to insure their gifts for future generations.

The Door Peninsula is blessed with over 600 state park campsites for those wishing to pitch a tent, roll out a sleeping bag or wheel in a recreational vehicle.

Despite the encouraging number of campsites, a camping trip to one of the state parks requires prior planning and often advance reservations. This is the rule rather than the exception during June, July and August, and the second weekend in October when Sister Bay hosts its annual fall celebration. Wisconsin state parks do not accept telephone reservations. You must make reservations in person at the park in which you plan to stay or by mail on an official state park reservation form. These forms are available at all Wis-consin state parks or from the Wisconsin Department of Natural Resources. To receive a free state park vis-itor guide and campsite reservation application write: DNR Parks, Box 7921, Madison, WI 53707, or call 608-266-2181. Photocopies of campground reservation applications are acceptable. Campsite reservations must be postmarked no earlier than the first working day of the year in which you plan to visit. Applications postmarked earlier will be returned. Reservations must be made for a two-night minimum stay (three nights on holiday weekends). A $3 nonrefundable reservation fee must accompany your application. For reservation periods refer to the information on the specific park you wish to visit.

If you plan to arrive by vehicle as most visitors do, you'll need a Wisconsin state park vehicle admission sticker. A vehicle admission sticker is not required to simply drive through the parks. However, if you park your car for any reason you'll have to pay the

LODGING, RETAIL AND RESTAURANTS

In 1980, there were 3,112 lodging rooms available in Door County. To-day there are over 5,100. Nearly one third of the restau-rants and almost 40% of the retail stores opened after 1980.

price of admission. Both daily and annual stickers are available, and the nominal fees are higher for non-residents.

Brown, Kewaunee and Door counties all converge on the Door Peninsula, adding a variety of county parks to a visitor's travel agenda. Of these natural areas, only Brown County's Bayshore Park offers camping facilities. Other county parks, however, merit attention for picnic areas, swimming beaches or grand vistas. Door County's Horseshoe Bay County Park, for example, offers a wonderful swimming beach, and Death's Door County Park affords an impressive view across the Porte des Morts Passage.

On Door Peninsula, taking a walk on the wild side means stretching your legs or pulling a paddle through one of the wild and rugged nature preserves. Thoughtful individuals and conservation organizations, notably the Nature Conservancy and Ridges Sanctuary, Inc., have preserved the biological diversity of the peninsula within untamed sanctuaries open to the public. These natural areas were chosen as delicate, pristine ecosystems that merit special attention.

Hiking the Door County Peninsula is one of the best ways to experience the diverse beauty this region offers. Hiking trails on the peninsula vary from gentle, easy strolls to strenuous backcountry rambles. While the peninsula lacks the long, isolated hiking stretches you often find in our national parks, it compensates with magnificent diversity and unique flora and fauna. Wildlife is abundant, and those willing to walk an extra mile or rise an hour earlier are sometimes rewarded with a fleeting glimpse of a ruffed grouse in flight or a coyote on the prowl.

With quaint country roads, cool lakeshore breezes, towering bluffs and shady swamps, biking Door County is wonderful. Whether you're a once-a-year pedaler or a weekend racer, you'll find bicycle routes to suit your style on the peninsula. Many of the trails recommended in this book have been designated bicycle routes by the Wisconsin Division of Tourism due to their scenic value and low traffic count. Automobiles are outlawed on the Sunset Bicycle Trail

BOUNTIFUL PARKLAND
Door County has five state parks and one state trail, more than any other county in the country.

and the Ahnapee State Trail. The other tours mapped, however, are regular county and state highways where you'll have to share the road with motor vehicles. Consideration on the part of both drivers and riders is necessary.

Quaint. Picturesque. Cozy. Historic. Door Peninsula communities have fought hard to avoid the blatant commercial tourist trappings that can plague vacation areas. Long providing a haven for artists, retirees and transplanted city folk, the people here are proud of their heritage, and eager to preserve it. Visitors will find a festival nearly every weekend in the summer. Autumn brings visitors to enjoy the vibrant fall colors. Winter brings ice fishing derbies, cross-country ski races and hot buttered rum.

World-class fishing opportunities await anglers visiting the Door Peninsula. The variety of bottom structure, the diverse shoreline and the variety of fish species present outstanding fishing action. The Wisconsin Department of Natural Resources has been stocking fish in the waters surrounding the Door Peninsula for nearly 20 years. Today their efforts are being rewarded with a legendary fishery that includes chinook salmon, lake trout, walleye pike, northern pike, whitefish, bass and perch.

Visitors without the knowledge, equipment or experience to pursue Lake Michigan salmon and trout by themselves will find charter fishing guides the most effective means of getting to Lake Michigan's trophy fishery. To hook up with a charter captain call the Door County Chamber of Commerce at 414-743-4456.

If you're planning to board a Lake Michigan charter, bring a day pack with warm clothing even in mid-summer. Once you're on Lake Michigan, cool breezes will be blowing and it's nice to have the comfort of a wool sweater and down vest. Rain gear is also advised. You'll need a Wisconsin fishing license, too. A daily fishing license is available, but usually not from the charter captain, so pick one up before you arrive. Beverages are usually available on board but you're welcome to bring your own on most charters. You'll want a cooler to bring your fish home.

MODEST DEVELOPMENT
Nearly 95% of Door County remains undeveloped. Development reaches its peak on the western shore of the peninsula, where planners are struggling to assure new construction is modest and environmentally sensitive.

7

The charter provides all your fishing gear and will fillet your catch.

The Wisconsin state record chinook salmon, a 43-pound, 3-ounce monster, was caught aboard an Algoma-based charter boat by a visiting Minnesota angler in 1983. With a little luck, the next record could be yours!

Meanwhile, walleye enthusiasts are hopeful the next state record for that species is swimming in Green Bay waters off the city of Sturgeon Bay. Lunker walleyes by inland lake standards are routinely caught in Sawyer Harbor and many fish biologists predict the best is yet to come.

Visitors who prefer not to board a Lake Michigan charter can simply drop a worm off a dock or shore and hope for the best. Many bass, perch, northern pike, salmon and trout are caught from Door Peninsula public docks and piers each year by visitors who have invested no more than the price of a rod, reel and lure or live bait.

A canoe, sea kayak or runabout will open the waters to many fishing opportunities. Protected bays, inland lakes and vast stretches of open water provide plenty of chances to land the fish of a lifetime, so cast luck to the wind and hope for a pole bender.

"Sweet water seas" is how the French Jesuit missionaries of the 1600s described the salt-free Great Lakes as they paddled their canoes along exploration routes that included the Door Peninsula. Today, touring kayakers part these same inland seas, upholding the tradition and sharing an ageless adventure.

The Door Peninsula hosted Wisconsin's first American Canoe Association sea kayaking workshop in 1987. The Peninsula State Park location inspired rave reviews from paddlers attending from across the Great Lakes. The peninsula's back bays, pleasing promontories and calm water coves welcome all levels of skill.

Canoeists heading for the peninsula can leave their river white water equipment behind unless they plan on playing in the lakeshore surf. Canoeing opportunities on the peninsula do not include white water rivers. Paddlers will not be disappointed, however.

ABUNDANT SHORELINE

Door County has more than 250 miles of shoreline. There are 92 public water access sites ranging from several miles, at state parks, to less than one hundred feet at road endings.

(opposite page)

Sea kayaking provides a peaceful retreat.

9

Secluded bays, inland lakes and even a fresh-water estuary rich in aquatic life greet visitors who arrive with canoes.

The peninsula has four inland lakes worthy of note for canoeists. Europe, Clark, Kangaroo and Mud lakes all afford public access with excellent canoeing opportunities. Inland lakes rarely prove threatening to canoeists and usually provide fishing opportunities to those wishing to wet their lines for panfish or the occasional northern pike or walleye.

Those looking for more challenging conditions will find open water paddling on both the bay side and lakeshore of the peninsula. Open water crossings are discouraged in an open canoe unless the weather conditions, waves and paddlers' skills combine for a safe outing.

Protected bays and shoreline paddling opportunities are almost unlimited. As a rule, the bay side of the peninsula generally offers greater protection, warmer water and somewhat smaller breakers than the lakeshore. But rules are made to be broken, and canoeists and kayakers looking for a calm-water tour might consider heading to the lakeshore when waves are battering the bay side. Kayakers wishing to play in the surf will find beautiful breakers at Whitefish Dunes State Park and Portage Town Park. The waves really begin building in September and October when wet and dry suits become standard equipment. Paddlers can find open water at Northport year-round, but in winter most kayakers agree the Washington Island Ferry is the best way to cross the whitecaps.

The peninsula's beaches are pure delight for those eager to catch some rays after a long, cold Wisconsin winter. You'll find beaches that vary from vast rolling sand dunes to white slivers just large enough to keep the waves from licking your heels. A trip to the peninsula is just not complete unless you come home with a pocketful of sand whether you visit in July or January. Winter brings its own special rewards to beachcombers who often discover winter waves carving castles of ice.

The Door County Peninsula has been called one of the top ten cross-country ski areas in the nation, and this may well be the case when the snow is deep and the trails are groomed. Unfortunately, snowfall on the peninsula varies dramatically from year to year and even from bay side to lakeshore. Mid-January through mid-March usually provides the best conditions. Early- and late-season skiers may wish to call the chamber of commerce snow condition hotline prior to their visit: 414-743-7046. The towering bluffs, the gorgeous views, the peaceful woodlands and the rolling fields are constants, however, and when winter cooperates they are unsurpassed.

Alpine skiers will find one ski area on the peninsula located at Potawatomi State Park. The slope has a moderate 120-foot vertical drop, but does boast a chair lift. Prices are reasonable.

Door County is a naturalist's delight. Make it yours. Whether you choose to make camp in southern Door County, on the Green Bay side or the lakeshore, or on one of the islands at the northern tip, you'll never be far from another adventure as you begin exploring the Door Peninsula.

SHORE TO SHORE

At its base the Door County Peninsula is about 18 miles wide, tapering to about three miles at its northern tip. The county contains about 475 square miles.

11

SOUTHERN
DOOR COUNTY

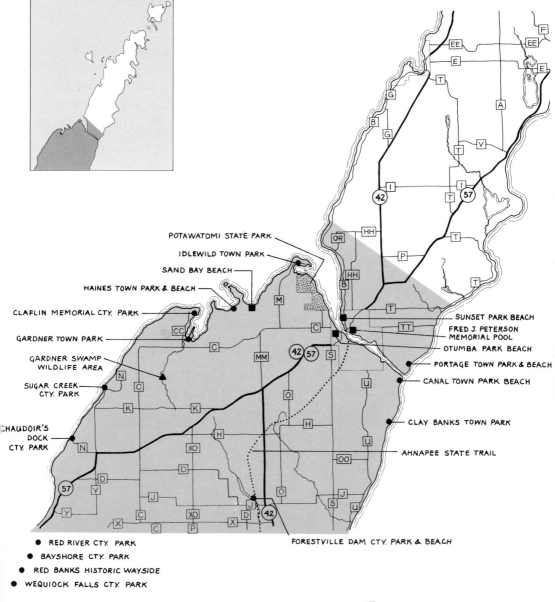

POTAWATOMI STATE PARK
IDLEWILD TOWN PARK
SAND BAY BEACH
HAINES TOWN PARK & BEACH
CLAFLIN MEMORIAL CTY. PARK
GARDNER TOWN PARK
GARDNER SWAMP
WILDLIFE AREA
SUGAR CREEK
CTY. PARK
CHAUDOIR'S
DOCK
CTY. PARK

SUNSET PARK BEACH
FRED J. PETERSON
MEMORIAL POOL
OTUMBA PARK BEACH
PORTAGE TOWN PARK & BEACH
CANAL TOWN PARK BEACH
CLAY BANKS TOWN PARK
AHNAPEE STATE TRAIL

FORESTVILLE DAM CTY. PARK & BEACH

- RED RIVER CTY. PARK
- BAYSHORE CTY. PARK
- RED BANKS HISTORIC WAYSIDE
- WEQUIOCK FALLS CTY. PARK

STATE PARKS
TOWN, VILLAGE & COUNTY PARKS
PRESERVES
BEACHES

Through the Windshield
AN OVERVIEW OF THE SOUTHERN DOOR

THE WHITE FATHERS

In 1893 the tiny community of Namur, in southern Door County, became the birthplace of the Catholic order of Norbertine priests in this country. The Indians called these priests "the white fathers." After their arrival from Holland, the Norbertines later established St. Norbert College in De Pere, a respected liberal arts college still in operation today.

(overleaf)

A young angler tries his luck off a Door County pier.

Rolling hills, dairy farms, and bayshore vistas usher visitors into Door County. Once considered a stepping stone to points further north, southern Door County is increasingly becoming a final destination for weary travelers. Captivated by its unpretentious rural atmosphere and reasonably priced shoreside accommodations, visitors are rediscovering this land once populated by Potawatomi and Winnebago Indians.

French explorers made many visits to southern Door County, taking advantage of its prominent location near the Fox-Wisconsin river watersheds and the Great Lakes trading routes. Today, visitors entering Door County via State Highway 57 arc across a geologic formation known as the Niagara Escarpment.

Wequiock Cascades County Park is an ideal location to take a close look at this rock outcropping. Here an exposed limestone ledge supports the tumbling water of Wequiock Creek. During the summer months this waterfall is little more than a trickle, but during spring runoff the flowing water creates a spectacular scene. Wequiock Creek terminates in a beautiful marsh as it enters Green Bay. This area, known as Point Au Sable, is prime waterfowl habitat. At low water this point offers beautiful white sand beaches accessible only by boat.

Continuing up the peninsula you'll get your first glimpse of the grand view overlooking a section of the Green Bay shore known as Red Banks. An historical marker and shoreside tablet here commemorate the visit of French explorer Jean Nicolet in 1634. Nicolet, an emissary of Governor Samuel de Champlain of New France, had been dispatched from Quebec to locate a convenient route to Asia. After paddling more than 1,000 miles through the Straits of Mackinac and on to Lake Michigan, Nicolet was convinced he had reached China. Landing on the Green Bay shore, Nicolet fully expected to meet the

14

Chinese and had brought along an elaborate Oriental robe specifically for that occasion. Donning the robe and emerging from his canoe, Nicolet fired two pistols in the air, much to the amazement of the Winnebago Indians who had come to greet him. Fascinated by the "thunder" he carried in his hands, the Winnebagos treated Nicolet and his crew to a banquet of "six score beavers." Soon, however, it was to be the pelt of the beaver and not its appeal to the palate that would be prized by the white men who followed Nicolet.

Just north of Red Banks, situated atop the Niagara Escarpment, stands Bayshore County Park. This Brown County park (listed separately) affords breathtaking views of the waters of Green Bay and offers 83 campsites amidst a wooded setting. A boat launching ramp (fee) provides excellent access to fishermen seeking perch and walleye in Green Bay waters. A pier provides fishing opportunities for those without a boat to test their angling skills. Park management does not encourage swimming off the park, but it's still a popular way to cool off on a warm summer day. Several spacious picnic areas are scattered throughout the park, complete with grills, picnic tables and a playground for children. A nature trail, softball diamond and shelter building combine to make Bayshore Park a popular spot for an hour or a weekend.

Continuing up the bayshore, travelers encounter the Kewaunee County community of Dyckesville. Residents of Belgian ancestry continue to celebrate the "Kermiss" here on the third Sunday in September, celebrating the harvest as they have for more than 75 years. Fishermen commonly frequent this bayshore village to stock up on bait, tackle and supplies for perch fishing. While the village itself lacks adequate public access to Green Bay waters, it is surrounded by a pair of county parks with public boat launching facilities. The second of these parks is Red River County Park, just north of the village. The Red River flows through this seven-acre park into Green Bay and includes 500 feet of bayshore frontage. A 40-foot summer "port-a-pier" and two boat-launching ramps provide access to the bay. The Red River sup-

CHERRYLAND BLOSSOMS

Door County has been called "cherryland" because it is the third-largest cherry-producing area in the nation. White cherry blossoms begin making their appearance in mid-May, followed by pink apple blossoms a week later.

ports a substantial smelt run in the spring, and dipping for the silvery fish is a popular evening activity when the "run" is on.

Crossing the Door County line, visitors will discover the village of Brussels (listed separately). Today few indications remain of the great "tornado" of fire that swept through this area in 1871. A wayside park north of the village marks the location where 60 persons perished at a community then known as Williamsonville. The villagers had sought refuge from the horrible inferno in an open field but were unable to escape the tremendous blaze. Nearby stands a well site that served as the last place of refuge for seven individuals attempting to escape the unbearable heat. The last man to crawl into the well pulled a wet blanket over the opening. Five of the seven desperate pioneers survived.

West of Brussels, a pair of county parks provides boaters with access to Green Bay. Fishermen will find an upgraded boat launch at Sugar Creek County Park (listed separately) and an emergency harbor of refuge for small boats at Chaudoir's Dock County Park (listed separately). Gardner Swamp Wildlife Area (listed separately) provides a nesting and resting location for both migratory and local waterfowl populations. This 1,000-acre preserve is open to the public year-round and provides opportunities for hiking, hunting, waterfowl observation and snowmobiling.

Visitors entering Door County via Highway 42 on the scenic Lake Michigan shoreline route will pass through the quaint Kewaunee County harbor communities of Kewaunee and Algoma, where it's easy to find a charter fishing captain anxious to add a passenger to his boat. Kewaunee takes its name from a Potawatomi Indian word meaning "we are lost." Apparently Indians paddling Lake Michigan would occasionally become disoriented amidst the deep fog on the lake while attempting to make their way back to shore. By shouting "Kewaunee" they alerted their friends on shore that they were lost and in need of direction. Today, Kewaunee's modern harbor employs sophisticated navigational equipment to aid the ferries that routinely shuttle commodities, passengers, and automobiles across the lake from Wisconsin to Michigan at a relaxing 18 miles per hour.

In the 1830s an unknown explorer discovered what he thought was gold at the mouth of the Kewaunee River. The ensuing "gold fever" didn't quite pan out and Kewaunee settled into a lumber economy. Today gold of a different sort is slated for collection from the Kewaunee River. The Wisconsin Department of Natural Resources is developing a new facility to collect and raise coho salmon and steelhead (rainbow) trout. These fish will then be used to stock Lake Michigan, adding to its trophy fishery. This developing fish collection facility will provide a viewing area so the public can get a closer look at the stocking program.

Traveling on to Algoma you'll find the site of another Potawatomi Indian village. Named "Wolf River" by early settlers, the town's name changed to Ahnapee, meaning gray wolf, in 1859. By 1897 the town had grown to 1,700. Then the name was changed to Algoma, or "Park of Flowers." This city's public harbor is undergoing extensive renovation that will include additional docking facilities. Sometimes referred to as "Penguin City," Algoma enjoys a summer climate substantially cooler than its northern neighbors, due to the chilling influence of Lake Michigan.

From Algoma, travelers with additional leisure time can continue north on County Trunk S along the lakeshore to County Trunk U. Frenchman Robert La Salle followed this route by canoe, camping on the southern Door lakeshore in 1679 before establishing a fur trading post on Rock Island. Robert La Salle County Park (listed separately) commemorates La Salle's visit and provides visitors with both shoreside access to Lake Michigan and a convenient picnicking location.

West of LaSalle County Park, on Highway J near Highway 42, Forestville Dam County Park (listed separately) provides canoe access to the slow-moving Ahnapee River. The Forestville Pond was formed by damming a portion of the Ahnapee during the late 1800s to provide hydro power for a gristmill. Frequently choked by aquatic weeds, the pond today does not provide the swimming and fishing opportunities it once did but it still provides excellent ac-

cess for mountain bikers wishing to shorten their ride
on the Ahnapee State Trail.

State highways 42 and 57 converge south of Sturgeon Bay near the access road to Potawatomi State Park. This forested preserve offers a modern 125-unit campground and opportunities for fishing, hiking, biking, skiing, and sight-seeing. Potawatomi offers the only downhill ski area on the peninsula, and an observation tower there provides an outstanding panorama of Sturgeon Bay and points beyond.

Arriving in Sturgeon Bay, it is clear from this community's relatively large size why it remains the center of government, commerce, and industry in Door County. Viewing its excellent harbor from one of the two bridges that span the bay, it's easy to visualize the attraction this area held for 19th century lumbermen anxious to harvest its virgin timber.

Father James Marquette was the first white man to record stopping at what is now Sturgeon Bay, in 1673. Following a portage trail blazed by the resident Indians, Father Marquette carried his canoe across the strip of land separating Green Bay from Lake Michigan. Today such a portage is no longer necessary. A ship canal, dredged in 1878 at the insistence of lumbermen, created a navigable channel uniting the waters of Green Bay and Lake Michigan at Sturgeon Bay.

HOME AND GARDEN WALK

Each July the Door County Hospital Auxiliary hosts a "home and garden walk" to highlight homes or buildings of particular interest or historical value. Contact the Door County Memorial Hospital (414-743-5566) for information.

STATE PARKS

Potawatomi State Park

Two miles south of Sturgeon Bay off Highway 42-57. Address: 3740 Park Drive, Sturgeon Bay, WI 54235. Phone: 414-743-8869.

FACILITIES:
125 campsites with electricity at 23 sites. Showers are available. Reservations are recommended during summer although some sites are kept available on a first-come, first-served basis. Open year-round.

RECREATION:
Hiking trails, fishing spots, downhill ski hill, cross-country ski trails, snowmobile trails, observation tower, boat ramp and biking opportunities.

A rugged, forested Green Bay shoreline greets visitors to Potawatomi State Park. Limestone cliffs give way to a rocky bay shore, and tall pine and birch trees sway in the wind.

Located as it is on the western edge of the city of Sturgeon Bay, Potawatomi State Park combines the convenience of city life with the isolation of a forest preserve. The park lies midway between the city of Green Bay, at the base of the Door Peninsula, and the village of Gills Rock, at the tip of Door County.

Many visitors to Potawatomi arrive in hopes of hooking a world-class walleye from the waters that surround the park. Others enjoy the spectacular vista from the observation platform that towers over the park. Bicyclists will find Potawatomi a convenient starting point for their further exploration of Door County. In fact, long-range park plans call for the development of a bicyclist camp for touring riders both here and at Newport State Park on the northern tip of the peninsula. Day hikers will enjoy the wildflowers and admire the white birch and red pine stands that provide cover for wildlife and renewal for trail trampers.

The park takes its name from the Potawatomi Indians who roamed this land when Jean Nicolet recorded a visit here in 1634. Sharing this land with the Potawatomi were other Woodland Indians, including the Fox, Chippewa, Menomonee, Sauk and Winnebago tribes. Native populations survived into the early 1800s, but gradually declined as white settlers staked their claims on the Door Peninsula.

The prominent limestone headland at the mouth of Sturgeon Bay above which the observation tower now stands has historically been known as Government Bluff. In 1834, the federal government began a rock quarry here, and Government Bluff was recognized not only for its commanding strategic view of both the Sturgeon Bay and Green Bay coastlines, but also for the high-quality limestone found beneath the shallow soil. In 1837 a 1,000-acre reservation was es-

POTAWATOMI STATE PARK

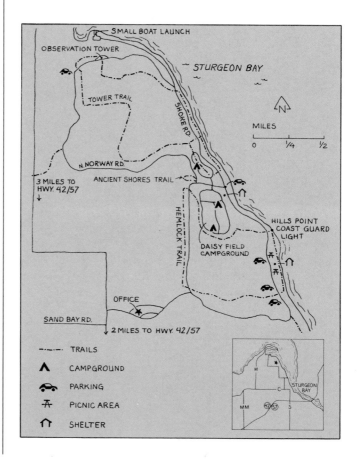

SMALL BOAT LAUNCH
OBSERVATION TOWER
STURGEON BAY
TOWER TRAIL
SHORE RD.
MILES
0   ¼   ½
N. NORWAY RD.
ANCIENT SHORES TRAIL
3 MILES TO HWY. 42/57
HEMLOCK TRAIL
HILLS POINT COAST GUARD LIGHT
DAISY FIELD CAMPGROUND
OFFICE
SAND BAY RD.
2 MILES TO HWY. 42/57

- - · - ·   TRAILS
CAMPGROUND
PARKING
PICNIC AREA
SHELTER

STURGEON BAY

(opposite page)

A small creek meanders through a garden of lady slippers enroute to its outlet at Lake Michigan.

20

tablished on the site, serving to isolate this area, much to the dismay of those early settlers who coveted both the natural and aesthetic resources of Government Bluff.

In 1928 the state of Wisconsin took an interest in the property and purchased the 1,046 acres at the mouth of Sturgeon Bay for $1.25 an acre. One year later a road was constructed through the "daisy field," up the bluff and around Sawyer Harbor. Two years later an observation tower was constructed that remains open to the public today, providing a sweeping panorama of Sawyer Harbor and beyond.

DAISY FIELD CAMPGROUND

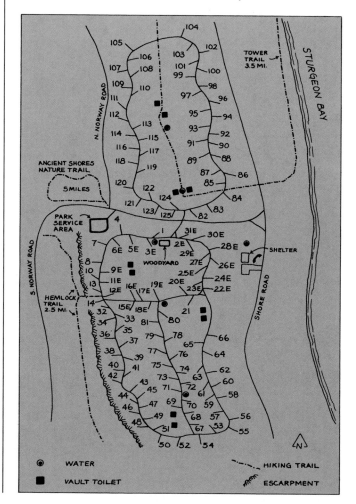

Today, visitors may be treated to a serenade from the more than fifty species of songbirds known to nest in or near the park. Hikers will find the dense forest filled with red oak, sugar maple, basswood and paper birch trees. Along the cliffs, white cedars are common. Spring is the best season for a wildflower hike, but many species will still be in bloom during the summer and fall as well. White-tail deer are commonly sighted, and raccoons, grey squirrels, opossums and chipmunks will be happy to treat themselves to your food cache if it's left unprotected.

Potawatomi State Park is also the eastern terminus of the Ice Age National Scenic Trail, which begins at the observation tower on Government Bluff. This 1,000-mile-long trail follows the edge of the furthest advance of the Wisconsin Glacier across the state. It dips southward from Door County before looping north and west to the banks of the St. Croix River. Although unfinished, the first part of the trail begins at the observation tower and follows Tower Trail through Potawatomi Park south along the shoreline and exits the park off Shore Road. Ice Age Trail symbols will guide hikers. The next major link in the trail occurs along the Ahnapee State Trail, which follows an abandoned railroad grade 15 miles to Algoma, Wisconsin. The connection between the park and the Ahnapee State Trail is not complete, but hikers can check with park rangers for the most convenient link.

Potawatomi State Park serves about 200,000 visitors annually. No doubt that number will increase now that shower facilities at the park's Daisy Field Campground are provided. This will also increase competition for the park's 125 campsites; reservations, especially for summer weekend campers, will become a necessity. Since only half of the park's campsites are reservable, visitors arriving without a reservation, especially mid-week, may still have a shot at securing a campsite for the evening. When the "no vacancy" sign is posted, you can have your name placed on a waiting list and play the campground shuffle. This requires that you meet at park headquarters the following morning at 10 a.m. At that time campsites are reassigned and campsite vacancies filled.

SHERWOOD POINT LIGHTHOUSE

Sherwood Point and its Coast Guard lighthouse take their name from Door Peninsula settler Peter Sherwood. Sherwood settled on the point in 1836, remaining until his death at the age of 80, in 1862. The Sherwood Point Lighthouse, situated on a bluff overlooking Sturgeon Bay, was built in 1883. The grounds are open to the public, and photographers will enjoy snapping a picture of this historic site.

After you set up camp it's time to plan activities. Potawatomi offers a full variety of interpretive programs for all ages. A naturalist might give a program about the animals or plant life in the park, or discuss the history or geology of the area. Programs are offered during June, July and August and are a good starting point for your exploration of the park. Check at the park office or on the park bulletin boards for times and places.

The steep cliffs and clear waters of Potawatomi make it a favorite oasis for day hikers as well as campers. Its proximity to the largest community on the peninsula make the trails attractive to local residents and visitors alike. The park is open year-round and many of the trails double as cross-country ski routes in the winter months.

HIKING TRAILS

Tower Trail: The trail head for the Tower Trail (3.5 miles) is reached by driving to the parking area atop the Potawatomi ski hill. This vantage provides a view of Green Bay waters to the north and rolling countryside to the west. Follow the trail north on the paved roadway along the highest bluff in the park to the observation tower. Once atop the tower, you'll be 225 feet above Sawyer Harbor, a popular year-round fishing spot. The trail continues south down a forested bluff to the shore of Sturgeon Bay. From here you'll wind through a cedar archway before making the gentle climb back to the trail head.

Hemlock Trail: Pick up the Hemlock Trail (2.5 miles) at parking lot 2 off Shore Road. The trail follows the service road to the picnic area along the shores of Sturgeon Bay, where fishermen are often spotted trolling for walleye pike, bass or trout. Crossing Shore Road, the trail bends north along the north side of the campground. After crossing Norway Road you will approach a field where summer brings the blooms of orange hawkweed, wild carrot and the yellow blossoms of common St. Johnswort. Crossing Norway Road a second time, you'll be hiking the interior of the forested park before cresting a limestone bluff and heading back down to Shore Road and the trail head.

Ancient Shores Nature Trail: Ancient Shores Nature Trail is a half-mile, self-guided route that begins across from the service area at the center of the park. The trail's 25 stations describe the plant and animal life as well as the geology and geography of the park. The trail takes its name from the two glacial lakes that once covered portions of the park, including what is now the Daisy Field Campground.

POTAWATOMI
WINTER
TRAILS

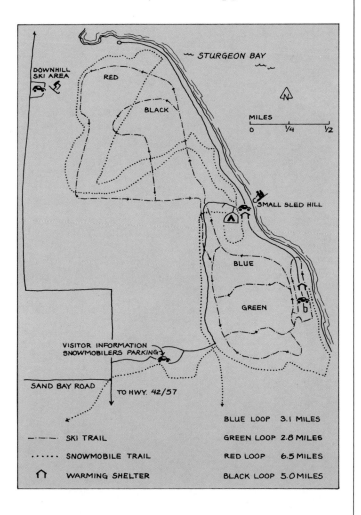

CROSS-COUNTRY SKI TRAILS

In winter, cross-country skiers can experience the same varied terrain and views of Sturgeon Bay on 13 miles of groomed trails. The trails are generally quite easy although there are a few hairpin turns that beginners may wish to avoid. The park is open year-round with a few campsites available for those willing to brave the elements.

The **red trail** (3.3 miles) is a park favorite, taking skiers along the highest bluff at Potawatomi before descending a gradual but exciting slope back to the Nordic warming shelter. En route you will pass the 75-foot-high observation tower, but the tower is not maintained by the park for winter use. Cresting the bluff you'll have a view of Sawyer Harbor below, and if you're tall enough, on a clear day you might see Menominee, Michigan, 18 miles away.

The pretty little **black loop** (two miles) shortens the red trail but still gives skiers a chance to experience the northern half of Potawatomi Park. Beginning at the warming shelter near the picnic area you'll follow the red trail before heading off on a one-way trail through the forest. This is a nice spot to decide whether you've got the time and energy to continue the extra 1.3 miles of the red loop. If not you'll descend to the camp area and the winter warming shelter.

The **blue loop** (3.1 miles) has been widened to an eight-foot corridor affording the best opportunities for skate skiing. Shufflers may wish to avoid this loop until provisions can be made to accommodate both styles of Nordic skiing on the same track. Beginning at the Nordic warming shelter near the picnic area, the blue trail follows the bay shore before creeping along the southwest side of the Daisy Field Campground. As you descend along the limestone bluff, use caution as you make the final approach to Shore Road and the warming shelter.

The **green loop** shortens the blue loop but still provides skiers with a scenic and interesting two-mile loop. Begin by following the bay shore briefly before connecting with the blue loop along the limestone bluff that circles back to Shore Road and the parking area.

(opposite page)

A cross country skier in full stride tackles a Door County trail.

27

DOWNHILL SKIING

Downhill and telemark skiers eager to stretch their muscles will find a modest 120-foot drop at Potawatomi State Park. The runs cater to beginners and experts alike with a double chair lift and two rope tows. A warming chalet offers a fireplace, snack bar and conversation with locals.

The entire operation at Mount Potawatomi is run by the nonprofit Potawatomi Park Ski Club. These dedicated volunteers keep lift tickets affordable even for large families. Snowmaking equipment helps keep the hill operating even during periods of only moderate snowfall.

Mount Potawatomi is open Saturdays, Sundays and holidays from 10:30 a.m. to 4:30 p.m. Lighted slopes allow night skiing each Wednesday from 6 to 10 p.m., weather permitting. For updated information and the price of lift tickets call the ski area: 414-743-7033, or Potawatomi State Park: 414-743-5123.

To get to the downhill ski area, exit Highway 57 south of Sturgeon Bay at Park Road. Follow the signs to Potawatomi State Park, but pass the park entrance and turn left (north) on Olson Road. Take Olson Road to Gitchee Gummee Road heading north to the ski area entrance. A state park vehicle admission sticker is not required to park at the downhill ski area.

TOWN, VILLAGE AND COUNTY PARKS

Wequiock Falls County Park *(2 acres)*

Located on Highway 57 at the southern end of the peninsula, this wayside park is situated on the Niagara Escarpment. Wequiock Creek cascades over the "ledge" in the spring, but slows to a trickle in the summer. Picnic tables and grates are provided, along with a first-hand look at the geologic formations that shape the peninsula.

Red Banks Historic Wayside *(1 acre)*

Located on Highway 57 north of Wequiock Falls stands an historic wayside paying tribute to Jean Nicolet, the first white man to land on the Green Bay shore, at a place called Red Banks. A bronze statue off the highway recalls Nicolet's visit. The wayside provides an excellent panorama of Green Bay waters.

Bayshore (Brown) County Park *(92 acres)*

The entrance is 15 miles north of Green Bay on Highway 57 and is well marked. Address: Route 1, New Franken, WI 54229. Phone: 414-866-2414.

FACILITIES:
There are 85 campsites, all available on a first-come, first-served basis. Water and flush toilets are operational about May 1, but pit toilets are available year-round. A camping fee is charged and there is a 14-day camping limit. Coin showers are available, and all campsites have electricity. Additionally, there is a laundry and a dumping station. No admission fee.

RECREATION:
The park has a boat ramp (a launch fee is charged), and there are short hiking and cross-country ski trails.

   An outstanding view of Green Bay from the Niagara Escarpment and a spectacular descent to the park's

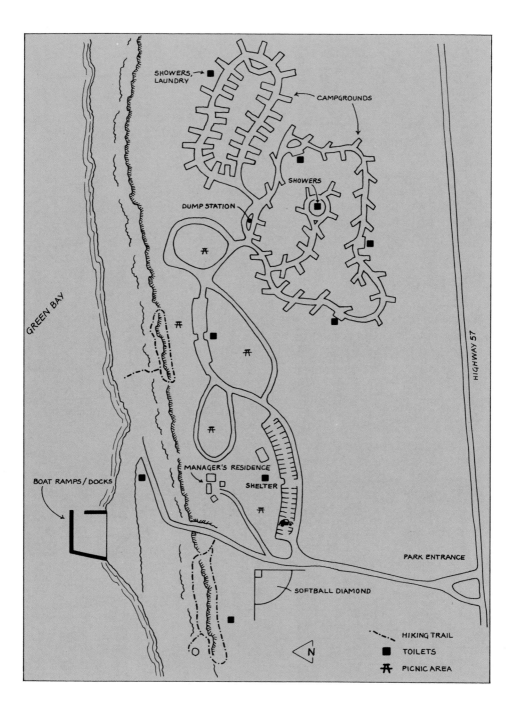

SHOWERS, LAUNDRY

CAMPGROUNDS

SHOWERS

DUMP STATION

GREEN BAY

HIGHWAY 57

BOAT RAMPS / DOCKS

MANAGER'S RESIDENCE

SHELTER

PARK ENTRANCE

SOFTBALL DIAMOND

N

HIKING TRAIL

TOILETS

PICNIC AREA

boat landing make Bayshore Park a pleasant resting place for travelers.

This park attracts fishing enthusiasts who launch their boats here in search of yellow perch. Several spacious picnic areas are scattered throughout the park for those wishing to grill some burgers while the children enjoy the playground. Nature trails, a baseball diamond, a volleyball area and a horseshoe pit also provide recreational opportunities. A shelter house on the park grounds may be rented year-round. The shelter has a fireplace, refrigerator, stove and picnic tables to seat about 70 people. Swimming is not officially condoned at the park but on a hot day it's tough to resist taking a dip.

(opposite page)
BAYSHORE COUNTY PARK

Camping is popular at the park's 85 wooded campsites, but since the park is open on a first-come, first-served basis, plan on setting up early or arriving midweek during the busy summer months. Since electricity is available at all campsites, this park is especially popular among RV campers.

The beautiful view from the edge of the cliff and convenient public access to Green Bay waters combine to make this park a favorite.

Red River County Park *(7 acres)*

The Red River flows through this seven-acre Kewaunee County Park north of Dyckesville. The park provides access to Green Bay waters with a boat launching facility. Picnic tables, grills, a shelter and privy are provided.

Chaudoir's Dock County Park *(5 acres)*

Located off Highway N, west of Namur, Chaudoir's Dock County Park offers two substantial docks serving as an emergency harbor of refuge for small boats. At times, the dock and nearby waters provide excellent fishing opportunities. The north dock was substantially improved in the fall of 1977 and is in excellent condition. The south dock is leased to a private party.

Haines Town Park *(2½ acres)*

You won't find any facilities at this Town Park, but who needs a picnic table when you've got a sand beach upon which to spread out your blanket? Located on Riley Bay, off County M, Haines Town Park is well protected from the wind, from all directions save west-northwest. Except for the beach, much of the area is wetland.

Tornado Memorial Park *(2.6 acres)*

This wayside park is located on Highway 57 about three miles northeast of Brussels. It was established to mark the location where 60 people lost their lives during the tragic Peshtigo fire of 1871. The park takes its name from the "tornado of fire" that leapt the waters of Green Bay to ignite the dry forests of Southern Door County. An historical tablet pays tribute to a handful of pioneers who survived the inferno by taking refuge in the nearby well that remains standing.

Sugar Creek County Park *(40 acres)*

Recently upgraded, this county park off County Trunk N offers an excellent boat launching ramp (fee) for fishermen seeking access to Green Bay. Those attempting to launch during poor weather should avoid this landing since the exposed bayshore is frequently buffeted by intense storms and the associated white-caps can be very intimidating. A large, wooded section of the park is entirely undeveloped and rustically appealing. Sugar Creek, for which the park is named, is popular with smelt dippers.

(opposite page)

A Great Blue Heron enjoys a fish dinner along the banks of the Mink River. Herons are frequently found spreading their wings above the sprawling wetland.

Gardner Town Park *(1½ acres)*

There are no facilities at this unmarked park that fronts the waters of Little Sturgeon Bay. Waterfowl appreciate this area because it is very low and marshy.

Claflin Memorial County Park *(.02 acres)*

Called a county park, Claflin Memorial Park is more accurately an historical marker commemorating Increase Claflin, who in 1835 became the first permanent white settler in Door County. Located off County Hwy CC, the site is identified by a low rail fence along each of its 28-foot-long sides. A large elm tree and a stone monument are framed by the fence. A picnic table and grill accommodate the occasional picnicker. The Door County Historical Society has officially recognized this locale as an historical site.

Idlewild Town Park *(6½ acres)*

Much of this park is low-lying and marshy. Located near the waters of Sawyer Harbor, on County Trunk M, Idlewild Town Park offers views of Potawatomi State Park and provides a scenic landscape to motorists.

Forestville Dam County Park *(79 acres)*

Once a popular fishing and swimming area, the Forestville Pond, choked by weeds and filled with rough fish, today does not provide an enjoyable experience for either use. The pond was formed by damming a portion of the Ahnapee River during the late 19th century to provide power for a gristmill. The dam, an earthworks piled across the river, has been repaired and rebuilt many times over the years. Recently the dam's spillway was completely rebuilt. The pond does attract waterfowl and has traditionally been a popular hunting area. This park has parking for about 15 cars and provides access for canoeists heading down the quiet water of the Ahnapee River. It is also located near the Ahnapee State Trail and mountain bikers can gain access here.

VILLAGE OF FORESTS

The community of Forestville was named during its heyday as a lumbering village. When the timber cutting came to an end in the late 1880s the stumps were cleared for farming. Today agriculture is the primary economy although second-growth woodlots continue to dot the landscape.

Robert La Salle County Park *(8 acres)*

This eight-acre park is distinguished by a three-tiered landscape consisting of pebble-strewn Lake Michigan shore, then a level, grassy upland area and finally a higher, wooded plateau. Steep sandy bluffs separate each tier. A stairway provides access to the middle and top tiers. The Door County Historical Society has erected a monument here, commemorating this park as a landing site of French fur trader Robert La Salle in 1679. A small stream cuts through an interesting sandy ravine along the southern side of the park. This park provides plenty of parking room and offers one of the few public access opportunities to Lake Michigan along the southern Door shoreline.

Clay Banks Town Park *(61 acres)*

Over three thousand feet of Lake Michigan shoreline comprise Clay Banks Town Park. This park is heavily wooded and boasts an excellent sand beach. You won't find any modern improvements to this park, but a road through this facility provides turnout parking opportunities for a few cars.

Sturgeon Bay Canal Town Park *(20 acres)*

Fishermen and naturalists share appreciation for this area. A breakwater pier offers a great view of the Coast Guard station while providing opportunities for anglers to try their luck at hooking a Lake Michigan trout or salmon. Naturalists will enjoy trying to identify the plants tenuously anchored to the deep sand found here. The narrow one-lane road leading to this park limits its use, so plan to arrive early if you're hoping for a parking space.

Portage Town Park *(20 acres)*

This historic town park is located just north of the Sturgeon Bay Coast Guard station on Lake Forest Park Road. A small tablet marks the entrance and commemorates the location where Indians once portaged their canoes from Lake Michigan to Sturgeon Bay. The park's wonderful sand beach attracts swimmers willing to brave the Lake Michigan chill, and surf casting for salmon and trout is a popular activity.

CLAY BANKS
Red banks of clay rise nearly one hundred feet from the Lake Michigan shore in the town of Clay Banks. Once a thriving trio of three villages, Clay Banks today is a single town dotted by farms and rustic lakeshore cottages.

PRESERVES

Gardner Swamp Wildlife Area

From Brussels, turn left (west) on County C. Follow C about three miles to Gravel Pit Road and turn right (east) into the area. Or, continue on C as it turns sharply right (east) to Pickeral Road. Turn right on Pickeral Road to Gardner Swamp.

FACILITIES:
Day-use.

RECREATION:
Hiking, bird-watching, hunting and snowmobiling.

Gardner Swamp Wildlife Area preserves 1,032 acres of swamp hardwoods and white cedar forest surrounding Keyes Creek. It provides a refuge for waterfowl, white-tail deer and an occasional green heron.

Located in the southwestern farm country of Door County, acquisition of land began in 1958. The need for this became apparent when beavers building dams on Keyes Creek continually flooded private land. During these periods it was noted that the beaver ponds held waterfowl, providing duck hunting opportunities. Thus, with the blessing of local landowners, state land acquisition was begun.

Spring-fed Keyes Creek is the only stream in the Gardner area. This five-mile-long stream flows north through the swamp to Little Sturgeon Bay on Green Bay. Keyes Creek develops into an expansive marshland on the property, and cattail, bulrush and sedge are found in low-lying areas of the swamp.

Gardner Swamp is an area of extreme importance to waterfowl on the Door Peninsula. Each year the area supports 30 to 40 broods of wood ducks, mallards and blue-winged teals. The area's close proximity to Green Bay and Lake Michigan also makes the swamp an attractive resting place for both migrating birds and visiting tourists in need of a rest break.

GARDNER SWAMP WILDLIFE AREA

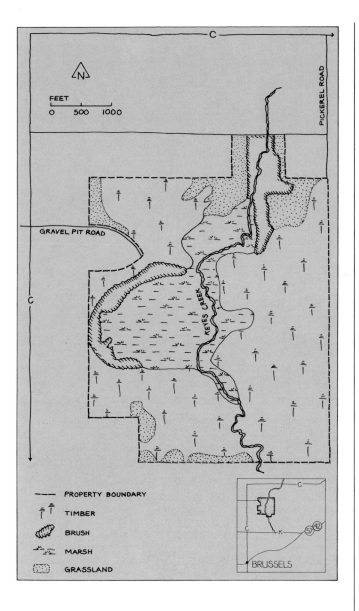

N

FEET
0   500   1000

C

PICKEREL ROAD

GRAVEL PIT ROAD

C

KEYES CREEK

- - - PROPERTY BOUNDARY

TIMBER

BRUSH

MARSH

GRASSLAND

C

K

57 42

BRUSSELS

BEACHES

Haines Town Park Beach

A sliver of sand about 12 feet wide and a great view await visitors at Haines Town Park Beach. Located on Riley Bay off Town Park Road, swimmers will find a shallow sand-bottom bay and a beautiful view of Snake Island in the distance. The beach is small but well protected from the winds on all sides except the west-northwest. A sign marks the park, and a small area is provided for parking. Excellent carry-in boat access is available.

Sand Bay Beach

Sand Bay Beach is an inviting, privately owned beach open to the public. This bay takes its name from comfortable sand that cushions the feet of swimmers as they saunter in for a swim. The resort beach offers a concession stand where ice cream and other summer staples can be purchased. The water here warms quickly, making Sand Bay Beach one of the best spots on the peninsula for a June swim.

Portage Town Park Beach

The beach at Portage Town Park is lovely. This out-of-the-way Lake Michigan beach attracts few visitors, which adds to its appeal. The water is frequently chilly, but somehow that seems bearable when the waves are crashing and the sun is high. This is an historical site, marking the location where Indians and fur traders carried their canoes from Lake Michigan to Green Bay waters. Access is off Lake Forest Park Road just north of the Coast Guard station.

Forestville Town Park Beach

The Forestville Pond once offered excellent swimming opportunities for bicyclists pedaling the Ahnapee Trail. That is no longer true. Choked with weeds

STRAWBERRY CREEK

Strawberry Creek, which flows into Sturgeon Bay near the shipping canal, was the site of Wisconsin's first chinook salmon planting, in 1969. Today, a condominium project and private marina are located near the mouth of this shallow creek.

and filled with rough fish, the pond is no longer the inviting swimming hole it once was. Public officials are concerned about this problem, and until improvements are made it's best to pass up this beach.

Sturgeon Bay Canal Park Beach

The city of Sturgeon Bay leases this beautiful 20-acre site from the Town of Sturgeon Bay for one dollar a year. You'll agree it's the best deal on the peninsula once you step onto the glorious beach that looks over the Coast Guard station at the mouth of Sturgeon Bay's shipping canal. A one-lane road leads to this beach, but parking is limited so plan to arrive early or pedal your bicycle to find a parking spot. To get to this hidden treasure, exit Highway 57 at County U and wind your way to the mouth of the shipping canal.

Sunset Park Beach

Sunset Park Beach offers swimming and the watchful eye of a lifeguard during specified times during the summer months, offering extra security for parents with small children. A bathhouse and restroom facilities make this a very popular "in-town" beach for visitors and locals alike. Access is off North Third Avenue (County B) from downtown Sturgeon Bay.

Fred J. Peterson Memorial Pool

A heated indoor public swimming pool named in honor of Sturgeon Bay shipbuilding magnate Fred J. Peterson is located near the shipyards on the city's east side. Showers and dressing rooms are available. Lifeguards keep an eye on the pool, which includes two diving boards. The pool is open seven days a week, including evenings.

Ottumba Park Beach

This Sturgeon Bay city park beach offers supervised swimming. Located near Potawatomi State Park, this

A fragile dune flower blossoms on the Lake Michigan shoreline.

beach offers excellent swimming opportunities lacking at Potawatomi. Restroom, playground and picnicking facilities are available.

La Salle County Park Beach

Robert La Salle County Park offers one of the few public access locations to take a swim in southern Door County. You'll have to make your way to the lower level of this three-tier park to reach the lakeshore. The park is named for explorer Robert La Salle, who landed here in 1679.

Canal End Town Park

There's a beautiful little beach here southwest of the shipping canal. From Highway 57 exit at County U to Lake. Turn left (east) to the beach and the 20-acre park.

STATE TRAILS

The Ahnapee State Trail *(15 miles)*

The Ahnapee State Trail follows an abandoned rail bed between Algoma and Sturgeon Bay. To get to the trail head at Sturgeon Bay, exit Highway 42-57 at County S south of the city. Take County S to Wilson Road. Turn left on Wilson Road and follow it to West Shiloh Road. The trail head at Algoma is one mile north of Algoma on County M.

AHNAPEE
STATE TRAIL

STURGEON BAY
C
~Shiloh Rd.
57
42
H — MAPLEWOOD
S
42
FORESTVILLE
J
— X —
D
M
—S—
ALGOMA

LAKE MICHIGAN

N

MILES
0   1   2   3

🚗 PARKING

WAYSIDE CHAPELS

A few wayside shrines or "praying chapels" remain scattered across the back roads of southern Door County. These small chapels date back to the days when roads were poor and churches were few and far between. Weary travelers once paused at these waysides to rest and pray.

The Ahnapee Trail follows the Ahnapee River, taking cyclists through a cedar swamp, past two villages and along the dairy farm country of Kewaunee County.

Once one of the finest bicycle tours on the peninsula, this trip is now best undertaken with a mountain bike. State budget cuts have eliminated trail maintenance, and until this situation improves the limestone screenings that make up the trail bed may have ruts capable of trapping narrow racing-style bicycle tires. Check first.

The Ahnapee was designated a National Recreation Trail in 1976. It now forms a link in the 1,000-mile-long Ice Age National Scenic Trail, which begins at Potawatomi State Park. Bikers and hikers share the trail spring through fall. In the winter the eight-foot-wide grade becomes a snowmobile trail maintained by local club members.

A movement is afoot to turn this trail over to an equestrian club for use as a bridle trail. They would be responsible for maintenance, but the trail would still be open to the public for hiking and bicycling under the proposed arrangement.

The Ice Age Trail

The observation tower at Potawatomi State Park marks the eastern beginning of the Ice Age Trail. Here one can climb the 225-foot tower while contemplating the glacial sheets that shaped this magnificent land 10,000 years ago. The last great episode of the Ice Age ended when an ice sheet, known as the *Wisconsinian,* crept into the state. The Door Peninsula, part of the Niagara Escarpment, split the advancing glacier into the Green Bay Lobe to the west and Lake Michigan Lobe to the right. Potawatomi State Park is situated on this limestone ridge, which extends from here to Niagara Falls.

Winding along a 1,000-mile pathway, the Ice Age Trail follows the hills, ridges, lakes and marshes carved by this glacial ice. Beginning at Potawatomi, the trail heads through Kewaunee and Manitowoc counties before reaching its southern terminus between Milwaukee and Madison. Winding north through central Wisconsin, the trail cuts west through the Northern Highland–American Legion State Forest and then to Interstate Park on the banks of the St. Croix River. The trail within Potawatomi follows the Tower Trail to the Sturgeon Bay shoreline, then continues south along the shore before leaving the park at Shore Road. Ice Age National Scenic Trail symbols mark the route from the tower.

To date about 350 miles of the Ice Age Trail have been established in segments ranging from two to forty miles in length. Development of this ambitious project began in the 1950s when Ray Zillmer of Milwaukee proposed a hiking trail that would follow the moraines marking the advance of the last glacier in Wisconsin. Zillmer, a Milwaukee attorney, loved to hike and, realizing the potential of combining nature study with outdoor recreation, began convincing others the trail had merit. Volunteers began building the first segment of the trail, and in October of 1980 Congress designated the Ice Age Trail a National Scenic Trail, one of only eight in the country.

Today a special Ice Age biking trail, sometimes coinciding with the Ice Age Trail and at times separate, stretches across Wisconsin. The Ahnapee Trail, just south of Potawatomi State Park, is one of these dual-use trails. It is important to note that the Ice Age Trail crosses both public and private land. Private landowners have given their permission to hikers to cross their property, provided they do so with care and consideration. Please respect their wishes. For more information on the Ice Age Trail contact: Ice Age Trail Council, 2302 Lakeland Avenue, Madison, WI 53704.

BICYCLE TOURS

Bayshore Breeze *(12 miles)*

This ride follows the Sturgeon Bay shoreline, then climbs a bluff northeast of the city before returning to the bayshore. This route shows off the developed area along the shore as well as country roads and

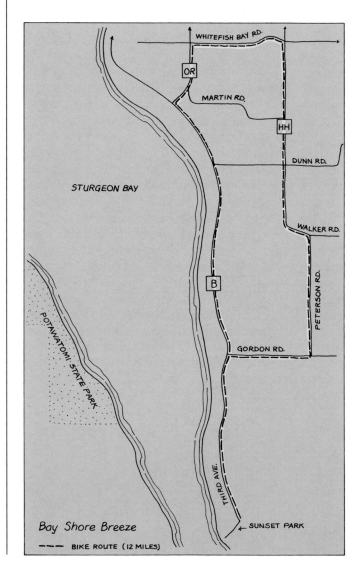

WHITEFISH BAY RD.

OR

MARTIN RD.

HH

DUNN RD.

STURGEON BAY

WALKER RD.

B

PETERSON RD.

POTAWATOMI STATE PARK

GORDON RD.

THIRD AVE.

← SUNSET PARK

Bay Shore Breeze

– – – BIKE ROUTE (12 MILES)

cherry orchards just outside the city of Sturgeon Bay. A swimming beach is available at Sunset Park, where this tour begins.

Beginning at Sunset Park at the north end of Third Avenue in Sturgeon Bay, head up the shore on County B (North Third Avenue). You'll immediately pass Little Lake, which is noted for its resident duck and geese populations. Potawatomi State Park is visible across the bay, and sharp-eyed cyclists might even locate the Sherwood Point Lighthouse in the distance. After traveling four miles, turn right on Old County OR and begin climbing the bluff. Looking back you'll be rewarded with a great view of the waters of Sturgeon Bay. Bear left at the intersection of Martin Road one quarter mile before turning right on Whitefish Bay Road. At the next stop sign turn right on County HH, making another climb up two small hills. On the crest of the bluff do not turn right but continue straight across Dunn Road until you reach the intersection of Walker Road and Peterson Road. Bear right on Peterson Road, descending down the bluff to Gordon Road. Turn right on Gordon Road and continue your descent across County HH and down to County Trunk B. Turn left and you'll find it's only a one-mile ride back to the beach at Sunset Park.

Ship Canal Clipper *(13.5 miles)*

This tour of the lakeshore crosses the portage trail that Indians once used to shuttle their canoes from Lake Michigan to Green Bay waters. You'll be traveling narrow, wooded lakeshore roads that provide access opportunities for swimming. Pack your swimsuit if you're brave enough to face the chilling waters of Lake Michigan.

Begin at the Sturgeon Bay Coast Guard station (follow the signs from Highways 42-57 at Sturgeon Bay). Turn right (north) leaving the Coast Guard station on Lake Forest Park Road. After one-quarter mile you'll reach an historical marker commemorating the portage trail. Portage Town Park is a great place to take a swim, but this is Lake Michigan so be prepared for a cool dip. Continue north on Lake Forest Park

Baileys Harbor is a popular spot to begin a bike ride to nearby Cana Island. The Ridges Sanctuary and Toft Point can be seen in the distance.

Road to County TT and turn right before making a quick left on North Lake Michigan Drive. This scenic, narrow road crosses County T where it becomes Brauer Road. Take Brauer Road to Forest Road and turn left. Continue past County View Road to Mathey Road and turn left on Mathey Road. Crossing County T again you'll see evergreen plantings by a Sturgeon Bay commercial landscape nursery. Whitetail deer enjoy these tender young trees and it's a constant battle to discourage them from munching on this profitable crop. Following Mathey Road across County TT you'll pass the Door County Rod and Gun Club before reaching Buffalo Ridge Trail. Turn right on this nicely wooded road and you'll pedal through a stand of birch, maple and evergreen trees. Passing Buffalo Ridge Road you'll reach Lake Forest Road. Turn right on Lake Forest Road and follow it past Portage Park and back to the Coast Guard station.

SHIP CANAL CLIPPER BICYCLE TOUR

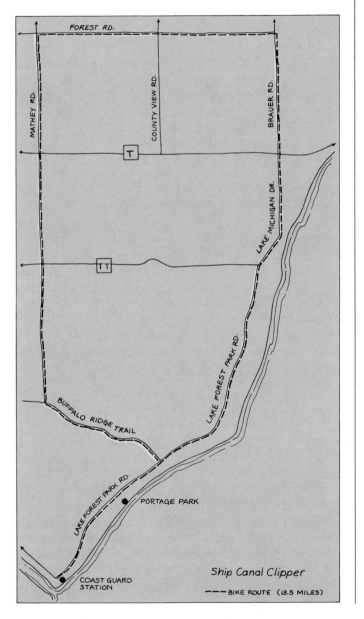

FOREST RD.

MATHEY RD.

COUNTY VIEW RD.

BRAUER RD.

LAKE MICHIGAN DR.

LAKE FOREST PARK RD.

BUFFALO RIDGE TRAIL

LAKE FOREST PARK RD.

PORTAGE PARK

Ship Canal Clipper

COAST GUARD STATION

――― BIKE ROUTE (13.5 MILES)

CANOE AND KAYAK ROUTES

Sawyer Harbor Swing

Summer and fall are the best times to explore Sawyer Harbor by canoe. The trip is best undertaken by those with an intermediate level of experience; it can take an hour or all day. Paddlers will find easy access, excellent fishing and interesting scenery despite development along Sawyer Harbor. Put in at the boat launch in Potawatomi State Park and either hug the Potawatomi park shoreline to the right (southeast) or head left (northwest) of the landing to explore the nooks and crannies of Sawyer Harbor while casting for northern or walleye along the shoreline. Homes and cottages line much of Sawyer Harbor's shoreline, but wooded wetland is also found, and the shoreline of Potawatomi is undeveloped. The unnamed islands in Sawyer Harbor are privately owned and trespassing is not allowed. Return to the boat landing and relax in the park before heading home.

Kayakers who take off around the harbor can take a break at the Sherwood Point Lighthouse across the harbor. Built in 1883, the lighthouse is no longer manned, but the grounds are open to the public. It's an interesting place to ponder the lonely life of a lighthouse keeper as you walk the grounds and admire the view. The navigation chart for the area is NOAA #14910.

Little Sturgeon Saunter

Keyes Creek finds an outlet at Little Sturgeon Bay and so do paddlers eager to put in a good workout. Exit Highway 57 west on County C at Brussels. Turn right on County CC and follow it to its conclusion. Turn right to get to Little Sturgeon Bay. The natural harbor off Green Bay is well protected but it pays to keep your eyes on the weather. It takes about an hour to explore the scenic coves along the jagged shoreline. If you want to stay on the water longer, Little Sturgeon Bay is one of the most popular yellow perch fisheries on the peninsula.

Ahnapee River Adventure

The Ahnapee is a meandering quiet-water river with some development. The marshy shore and farm fields provide a quiet rural setting. To get to the put-in at Forestville Dam Park, exit Highway 57 south of Sturgeon Bay at Highway 42. Head south to Forestville, then right (west) on County J to Forestville Park. The trip down the river takes a full day since a shuttle return is required.

The Ahnapee River follows the Ahnapee State Trail as it meanders through southern Door and northern Kewaunee counties. Paddlers are likely to startle waterfowl, and quiet observers may happen upon whitetail deer along this route. The murky water is home to northern pike and a spring and fall run of steelhead trout. The take-out for this trip is at Olson Park near the intersection of Highway 42 and County S in Algoma. Ample parking is available. A bike shuttle is also possible via the Ahnapee State Trail if you feel secure leaving your bicycle locked at the put-in. Try this paddle in early fall.

Portage Park Paddle

Kayakers can put in at Portage Park immediately north of the Sturgeon Bay Coast Guard Station on Lake Forest Park Road on the Lake Michigan side of the peninsula. When the waters are calm beginners can handle this, and on stormy days kayakers wanting a little lakeshore white water will be pleased to find a rolling surf here as waves torment the beach. If it's quiet water you're in search of, head to the bay side of the peninsula.

The sandy beach provides a convenient put-in for a flat water summer cruise as well. To your immediate right, the Coast Guard pier guards the ship canal. This man-made passage to Sturgeon Bay provides passage to Green Bay waters if you're up for a major cruise. Heading left (north) up the coast you'll pass a nice collection of summer homes; during autumn, residents can sometimes be found surf casting for steelhead trout.

CITIES, TOWNS AND VILLAGES

Sturgeon Bay *(pop. 9,118)*

Sturgeon Bay stands as gatekeeper to the northern Door Peninsula, requiring all who pass to admire the beautiful view this natural harbor presents from the two bridges that connect the two sides of the city.

The city takes its name from the ancient giant fish species that was once so prevalent in these waters that in winter, settlers would stack five-foot-long sturgeon on the dock like cords of wood. Sturgeon no longer ply these waters, having disappeared under the same stresses of modern life that also claimed the Indian settlements that fished here prior to the white man's arrival.

The rich modern history of Sturgeon Bay begins with Father Jacques Marquette, a Jesuit missionary who in 1673 was the first white man to record a visit to this bay. Using an Indian portage trail, Marquette spent two days shuttling his canoe and supplies one mile overland from Green Bay to Lake Michigan near where the present-day ship canal divides the city of Sturgeon Bay. Portage Town Park acknowledges this trail and its colorful past.

A county park south of here marks the historic site where seven years later four members of an ill-fated expedition survived the winter thanks to the aid of friendly Indians. Local history has it that the group was a remnant of Frenchman Robert La Salle's first (and disastrous) expedition that fled an Indian mutiny at Fort Crevecoeur near the headwaters of the Illinois River. Having landed their canoes, the party apparently struggled over the Sturgeon Bay portage and paddled 14 miles up the bay shore to Egg Harbor. Weak and tired, the group sat out a five-day November sleet storm at Horseshoe Bay, consuming even their leather moccasins for nourishment. Void of supplies and low on hope, they returned to Sturgeon Bay where they had seen dry wood, "that they might die warm," according to expedition member Henri de Tonty. It was here that Onanquisse, a mighty Pota-

SHIPBUILDERS

The Sturgeon Bay shipping canal, completed in 1878 and linking the waters of Green Bay with Lake Michigan, paved the way for Door County's shipbuilding industry. In 1897 a commercial drydock was built at Sturgeon Bay, providing the foundation for the city's shipbuilding industry. Production increased dramatically during World War II, and today the construction of military ships and luxury yachts is still a mainstay of the Sturgeon Bay economy.

watomi Indian chief, showed mercy, offering the pit-
iful group food and shelter that insured their survival.

Over 200 years later in 1878, the portage trail became obsolete when a ship canal, visible from the
city's bypass bridge, was blasted through the limestone rock, permanently uniting the waters of Lake
Michigan and Green Bay at this point. Still in use
today, the canal provides mariners a shortcut through
the Door Peninsula and eliminates the treacherous

*Ancient sand dunes
anchor rare plants at
the mouth of Sturgeon
Bay's ship canal.*

51

journey through Death's Door Passage at the tip of the peninsula.

In 1858, Switzerland native Joseph Zettel acquired a farm about four miles north of Sturgeon Bay and established the first commercial orchard on the Door Peninsula. Zettel's high yields and quality fruit spurred the interest of professors at the University of Wisconsin, who concluded that the peninsula is remarkably well suited to fruit growing. Commercial production of red cherries began in 1896, and in 1922 the University of Wisconsin established a 120-acre fruit research station here.

The Door Peninsula continues to produce the third-largest cherry crop in the nation, cultivating the Montmorency variety of red tart cherries. Orchards here also produce 40% of Wisconsin's apple crop. Mid- to late May finds the fruit trees in bloom, and orchards of pink and white blossoms dot the landscape. Mid-July is cherry-picking time and visitors are welcome to pick their own cherries in many orchards. After the harvest, fruit stands cater to visitors, selling frozen cherries to use in your favorite recipes.

History buffs will enjoy Sturgeon Bay's downtown district. A tour map, available at the city's information booth, will guide you along the city's two districts listed in the National Register of Historic Places. You are welcome to walk, bike or drive the tour, which includes 100 buildings.

Sturgeon Bay remains the center of commerce, banking and industry on the Door Peninsula. Its boom-and-bust shipbuilding industry continues to be a major source of employment, though the city is constantly expanding and diversifying its industrial base. Tourism is an important industry, and accommodations in the city range from quaint bed-and-breakfast inns and rustic cabins to modern hotels.

Door County Library: 4th and Nebraska Sts. This is a full-service library with an interesting local history collection housed in the Laurie Room.

Miller Art Center: 4th and Nebraska Sts. This gallery is located in the Door County Library and boasts an excellent collection of paintings by Door County artists.

SAWYER NAMED AFTER ITS POST OFFICE

The tiny village of Bayview was platted in the late 1870s, but locals called it "Sawyer," after its post office. A narrow strip of water separated what was then Sawyer from Sturgeon Bay, creating a communication and commerce barrier between the two communities. In 1887 a private toll bridge linked the communities during the summer months, while ice provided a natural bridge during winter. In 1891, the two communities established a permanent link when the state legislature consolidated Sawyer as the fourth ward of the City of Sturgeon Bay.

Door County Museum: 4th and Michigan Sts. This museum's emphasis is Door County's ethnic past, including the peninsula's Belgian, German and Scandinavian heritage.

Peterson Memorial Pool: 207 S. 3rd Ave. Residents and visitors alike may enjoy swimming in this indoor year-round facility. It's named for shipyard entrepreneur Fred J. Peterson.

Lawrence Big Hill Park: Off 9th Ave. from Rhode Island St. The view makes this a great place for a picnic.

Garland Park: Off Business 57 across the bay. This two-acre, pleasantly wooded park is nice for an in-town picnic.

Martin Park: This park on S. 3rd Ave. has picnic tables and a band pavilion.

Little Lake Park: Off N. 3rd Ave. This borders Sunset Park and has a 24-acre lake stocked to provide fishing for children. Tame ducks live here, so be on the lookout as you drive in.

Bay View Park: This park has a nice view of the shipyards from the west side of Sturgeon Bay.

Memorial Field: Off Michigan Ave. at 12th St. This lighted athletic field hosts major local sports events.

Sunset Park: N. 3rd Ave. A popular in-town swimming beach and picnic grounds are located here. A lifeguard is on duty at specified times.

Ottumba Park: On Juniper St. on the west side. There is a swimming beach and a picnic ground here. A lifeguard is on duty at specified times.

Canal End Town Park: There's a beautiful little beach here southwest of the shipping canal. From Highway 57 exit at County U to Lake. Turn left (east) to the beach and the 20-acre park.

Portage Town Park: Just northeast of the Coast Guard Station off Lake Forest Park Road, this historic park has a nice small beach.

Door County Chamber of Commerce: Box 346, Sturgeon Bay, WI 54235. Phone: 414-743-4456. The office is located just south of Sturgeon Bay on Highway 42-57.

Sturgeon Bay Information Center: P.O. Box 212, Sturgeon Bay, WI 54235. Phone: 414-743-3924.

Robert de La Salle County Park: Due east of Brussels on Lake Michigan. Access is off County U just south of County J. This 80-acre park offers a nice view of Lake Michigan as well as a pebble beach. There are facilities for picnicking.

Forestville Dam County Park: Southeast of Brussels on the Ahnapee River. Take County J to the park, which is just past the intersection with County D. The park is adjacent to the Ahnapee State Trail and is a nice place for a picnic.

Chaudoir's Dock County Park: West of Brussels off County N. This small park offers a boat launch onto Green Bay and picnic facilities.

Haines Town Park: This 2.5-acre park is off Town Park Road north of County C at Riley's Bay. There is an unimproved small boat landing and a small beach.

Tornado Memorial Park: This is a wayside with picnic opportunities on Highway 57 north of Brussels.

Sugar Creek County Park: Access to this park is off County N on Green Bay. It's possible to launch small boats here. The park covers about 40 acres.

Gardner Swamp Wildlife Area: Six miles northeast of Brussels. Take County C to Gravel Pit Road. There are hiking paths and public hunting in season for deer, ruffed grouse and waterfowl in this 1,032-acre preserve.

Brussels *(pop. 1,159)*

Tidy farms and rolling hills contribute to the scenic rural landscape surrounding the village of Brussels. The village center is nothing more than a supermarket and a pair of feed mills, but the community is actually made up of hearty farmers, most of Belgian ancestry, who cling to the hard work ethic passed on by their forefathers.

Amid the farms and fields of southern Door and bordering Kewaunee and Brown counties, visitors will find one of the largest Belgian settlements in America. Many of these folks still speak the native languages of their grandparents, either French or Walloon. Even when the residents speak English, visitors are likely to note a dialect unique to this part of Wisconsin. For instance, a local shopper may request "smashed meat" instead of hamburger at the corner supermarket.

The first Belgian immigrants carved their homes and farms from the forested wilderness surrounding the hamlet of Champion near the southern end of the peninsula. Letters to their relatives back home promising a land of timber and farm fields brought a wave of immigration in the mid-1850s.

Today, backroad travelers will find evidence of this early settlement when they visit the tiny, close-knit communities of Thiry Dames, Rosiere and Walhain.

The surprising number of red brick farmhouses that dot the highway, especially between Namur and Brussels, can be linked to the devastating Peshtigo Fire of 1871. During the fall of that year the logged-over bay shore woods was a tinderbox due to a hot, dry summer. As isolated fires burned in the cutover, smoke and ash rained down on Green Bay. Then, on October 8, one day prior to the Great Chicago Fire, strong winds fanned separate flames, creating an immense pillar of fire that was described as a "tornado of flames." Before the disaster was complete, 1,200 people had perished and whole villages were destroyed on both sides of the bay shore.

The Peshtigo Fire left in its wake about 5,000 homeless Belgian immigrants. It seemed their American dream had ended. But with help from their southern neighbors these hearty settlers rebuilt. They replaced their wood frame homes with brick structures that would be better able to withstand a second inferno, which, thankfully, has never arrived.

To celebrate its ethnic heritage, Brussels holds its annual Belgian Days Festival the second weekend in July. It's a great time to explore this area and enjoy some Belgian tripe (a Belgian sausage made from pork and cabbage) and Belgian pies.

ROBINSONVILLE CHAPEL

The Belgian community of Champion marks the location where many contend the "Queen of the Heavens" appeared to a young farm girl named Adele Brice during the 1860s. Adele was instructed to "Gather the children of this wilderness and teach them what they need to know about salvation." This lovely and mysterious chapel is thought to be the site of many divine miracles. Today, the hall of the sacristy is filled with canes and crutches left by those cured of their afflictions.
Hundreds gather from across the world each August to celebrate the Feast of the Ascension in a grand procession that winds through the church grounds.

BAYSHORE

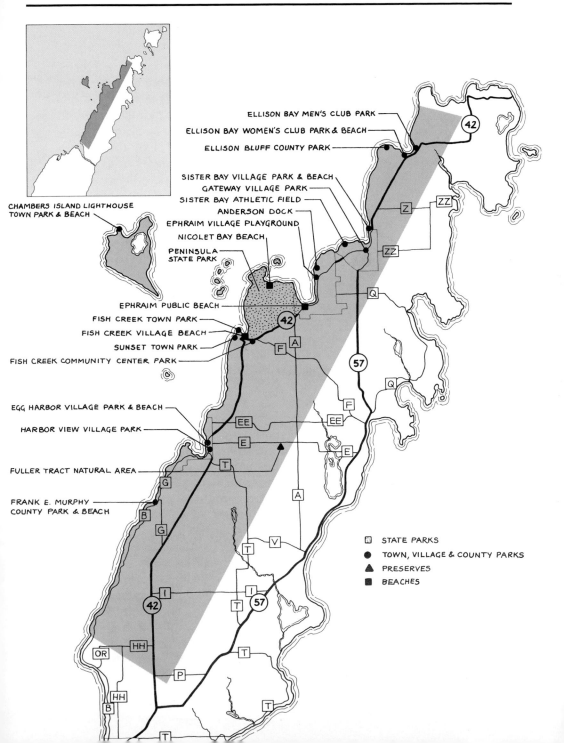

ELLISON BAY MEN'S CLUB PARK
ELLISON BAY WOMEN'S CLUB PARK & BEACH
ELLISON BLUFF COUNTY PARK

SISTER BAY VILLAGE PARK & BEACH
GATEWAY VILLAGE PARK
SISTER BAY ATHLETIC FIELD
ANDERSON DOCK
EPHRAIM VILLAGE PLAYGROUND
NICOLET BAY BEACH

CHAMBERS ISLAND LIGHTHOUSE
TOWN PARK & BEACH

PENINSULA
STATE PARK

EPHRAIM PUBLIC BEACH
FISH CREEK TOWN PARK
FISH CREEK VILLAGE BEACH
SUNSET TOWN PARK
FISH CREEK COMMUNITY CENTER PARK

EGG HARBOR VILLAGE PARK & BEACH

HARBOR VIEW VILLAGE PARK

FULLER TRACT NATURAL AREA

FRANK E. MURPHY
COUNTY PARK & BEACH

STATE PARKS
TOWN, VILLAGE & COUNTY PARKS
PRESERVES
BEACHES

Through the Windshield
AN OVERVIEW OF THE BAYSHORE

Bayside beaches and waterfront campsites bring thousands of visitors each year to Door County's western shore. The reason they arrive is as varied as their backgrounds, but it seems all are seeking the serenity of a sunset or the comfort of a sandy beach.

The bayshore is considered by many the cultural center of Door County. The summer brings professional theatre, music, dance, art, and education to its shores. The villages bustle with activity but those seeking peace and quiet can still find a quiet cove in which to relax.

To travel north from Sturgeon Bay, visitors can select either County Trunk B along the bayshore or State Highway 42. Both roads intersect at Egg Harbor but the scenic bayshore route rewards drivers and bicyclists with stunning views at the expense of slower travel. To travel this route, head north on 3rd Avenue (County B) from downtown Sturgeon Bay where you'll pass Sunset Park. This attractive city park has a lifeguard-patrolled sand beach and boat launching ramp. Be on the lookout for ducks crossing the road at adjacent Little Lake. Little Lake is a scenic pond with city parkland surrounding its shores. This lake is stocked with fish for the enjoyment of pint-sized anglers. Continuing north you'll find the remnants of an old limestone quarry.

If you're longing for a swim or are anxious to get your kayak in the water, you'll be pleased to discover the next point of interest on your bayshore drive. Frank E. Murphy County Park (listed separately) has a great sand beach with excellent swimming opportunities. This park is very popular with local families, and after a refreshing dip, you'll understand why. The bluff opposite Murphy Park holds Tecumseh Cave, the longest cave in Wisconsin. The entrance to this cave is private, however, and exploration is prohibited. From Murphy Park it's less than three miles to the Village of Egg Harbor. This once-sleepy community is experiencing rapid growth, but planners

(overleaf)

The natural harbor of Peninsula State Park's Horseshoe Island is a popular destination for sailors, sea kayakers and canoeists. Whitetail deer have been sighted swimming from the island to the mainland.

are taking care to maintain its unique charm.

Travelers departing Sturgeon Bay on Highway 42 will see farm fields and rural scenery as they head through the heartland of Door County. Unfortunately, zoning restrictions have not kept pace with lodging demands. Scattered developments are beginning to take their toll on the landscape. Sensitivity to this situation is on the rise, however, and unsightly developments are being met with increasing opposition.

If you're interested in the agricultural past and future of Door County, you'll wish to pause at the University of Wisconsin Agriculture Experiment Station on Highway 42, just past the junction of State Highways 42 and 57. The Peninsular (correct spelling) Experiment Station was established in 1922 when the University of Wisconsin purchased the John Kruzich Farm. This station is one of ten experimental stations maintained by the University. These units allow researchers to take their experiments from the laboratory to the field and make evaluations under the differing climate and soil types of Wisconsin. Even if the station is closed, you'll find an interesting state historical marker recalling the history of the Door County orchards. The land just south of here became the first commercial orchard on the peninsula when Switzerland native Joseph Zettel began farming the land in 1858. The highway pulloff provides a convenient place to stretch your legs while reading the bronze tablet. If you're interested in a swim, exit Highway 42 at County G for a trip down the ledge to Frank E. Murphy County Park before heading into Egg Harbor.

The Village of Egg Harbor is nestled in a protected harbor on Horseshoe Bay. A pair of village parks afford access to the harbor and pleasant views of Horseshoe Bay. White Cliff Road follows the bayshore beside a striking cliff after which the road takes its name. This road parallels Highway 42 up to the small community of Juddville. Although most visitors travel Highway 42, White Cliff Road will not disappoint those seeking a colorful fall route when the leaves are brilliant and the air is crisp.

Sidetracking on County E, east of Egg Harbor, you'll encounter the Peninsula Center Sanctuary, also known as the Fuller Tract. A stone marker identifies the boundaries of this 160-acre preserve, which serves as a University of Wisconsin natural area. Continuing on County E, the road crosses a causeway dividing Kangaroo Lake before ending at Highway 57 just south of Baileys Harbor. Kangaroo is a 1,100-acre lake deriving its water from a spring-fed stream. The causeway separating the lake provides public fishing and boat launching opportunities. A small public swimming beach can be found at the end of Beach Road on the western shore of the lake. (The water in Kangaroo is typically much warmer than either Green Bay or Lake Michigan.) A small boat launch is available at the end of O'Brien Road. Sand dunes separate the eastern shore of Kangaroo from Lake Michigan and add to its scenic value. Although Kangaroo Lake is dotted with cottages and resorts, its clear water and appealing wetlands make exploration by canoe or small sailboat most inviting.

Departing Egg Harbor on Highway 42 at Juddville, you'll encounter the access road to the Peninsula Players' "Theater in a Garden." The bayshore setting and the wooded garden provide an outstanding backdrop in which to enjoy the delightful performances of this professional summer resident theater troupe. This is the best nightspot on the peninsula as the sun sets over Hat Island on the horizon and playgoers are ushered to their seats. The all-weather pavilion allows the show to continue rain or shine and the affordable ticket prices bring visitors back year after year.

Descending the bluffside curve on Highway 42, you'll enter the lively community of Fish Creek, gateway to Peninsula State Park. This 3,700-acre park is the most popular attraction on the Door Peninsula, and justifiably so. The park is actually a spectacular peninsula on a peninsula, encompassing all of the bayshore property between Fish Creek and Ephraim. Established in 1910, the park protects seven miles of Green Bay shoreline comprised of towering limestone bluffs, rich wetlands and second-growth northern forests. The park is a popular destination for campers, but reservations are almost mandatory during the heat of summer and the color of fall.

During the summer you'll find a festival nearly every weekend in Fish Creek. The streets of this village are usually bustling with activity. During the off-season, however, the town is deserted and many seasoned visitors time their vacations to take advantage of this relaxed pace. In the village center along the bayshore, Fish Creek Town Park overlooks Peninsula State Park. This park is the center of activity during the many festivals the village hosts, and the public dock here attracts skippers from throughout the Great Lakes. Many captains start their voyages to Chambers Island from this village.

Chambers Island is located about five miles northwest of Fish Creek, in the shadow of the Strawberry Island Chain. The Strawberries, as they are called, consist of four small, privately owned islands: Adventure, Jack, Pirate, and Little Strawberry. The treacherous reefs surrounding this chain make development of the islands difficult, enhancing nesting opportunities for shore birds.

Beyond the Strawberry Islands, lake swells can become threatening, and boaters making their way to Chambers Island should use caution. Chambers Island is a remote and beautiful privately owned island about two and one half miles wide by four miles long. It was named in 1816 in honor of Colonel Talbot Chambers, a soldier dispatched from Mackinac and appointed the task of establishing a military post here.

A lighthouse on the island began operation in 1868 and was serviced by nine lighthouse keepers, with the last retiring from his lonely post in 1950. These lighthouse keepers saw many changes come to the island. In the 1920s a syndicate called the Chambers Island Association had the island surveyed with plans to create an exclusive vacation retreat for the wealthy. The 2,500-foot airport runway that was cleared for the development remains in use, but the golf course has since overgrown. When the stock market crashed, so did the Chambers Island development project. By

POW CAMPS

During the summer of 1945, a German prisoner-of-war camp was located in Fish Creek. Prisoners did construction jobs, wood cutting and cherry picking within Peninsula State Park and the surrounding area.

1933 all the island's real estate owners went into bankruptcy, and three years later Door County divided and sold the island to private individuals to satisfy back taxes.

Today, the Town of Gibraltar maintains a forty-acre park located near the lighthouse on the northwest side of the island, and boaters frequently throw out an anchor to enjoy the inviting sand beach found here. A Catholic retreat house is located on the island, built on a sand isthmus separating the waters of Green Bay from inland Lake Mackaysee. This 354-acre lake is one of two inland lakes on Chambers Island.

Mackaysee, with a depth of 26 feet, is the deepest inland lake in Door County. It is an ancient glacial lake of striking natural beauty known for its bass, bluegill and northern pike fishing. There are a pair of islands in the lake, and very little development mars the scenic shore. About thirty acres of wetlands adjoin Lake Mackaysee, providing a nesting and resting spot for waterfowl. Unfortunately, there is no public access to this scenic beauty.

The second inland lake on Chambers Island is little more than a four-acre pond known as Krause, Mud, or Lost Lake.

Back on the mainland, it's only a short walk from the Fish Creek dock to Sunset Town Park. If you wish to see the sunset over the bay, this is the place to do so. To reach this small park follow the wooded grove past Founders Square on the western edge of town.

Backtracking through the village center you'll find the Fish Creek Village Beach. During summer this is a center of activity. A marked swimming area and sand bottom offer excellent swimming opportunities. Just north of the beach the creek for which the village is named is crossed by Highway 42. The creek originates in swampland and flows into Green Bay, forming the southwestern boundary of Peninsula State Park for a distance of about 1,000 feet. The stream is intermittent but at times a canoe can be paddled from Green Bay upstream. The northern shores of this stream have been protected as parkland and the southern shores merit similar protection.

Departing the village of Fish Creek you'll be climbing a hill and making a sweeping curve past the Town of Gibraltar school grounds. The high school auditorium is the site of the annual Peninsula Music Festival. Each August this three-week series of classical music concerts attracts both musicians and visitors from throughout the country. It was founded by the late Dr. Thor Johnson, conductor of the Cincinnati Symphony Orchestra. A fund drive is underway to improve and expand this auditorium into a 750-seat school and community facility.

Continuing on Highway 42, you'll find the southeastern border of Peninsula State Park providing a visual oasis as you travel from Fish Creek to Ephraim.

A young visitor checks out the bay shore from Fish Creek's Sunset Town Park. Chambers Island is visible in the background.

Reaching the northern entrance of Peninsula State Park, you'll encounter a championship-caliber 18-hole golf course complete with a pro shop and restaurant. A state park sticker is not required to park at the course but golf reservations are recommended during July and August.

Winding into Ephraim you'll enjoy your first view of Eagle Harbor. This well-protected bay affords swimmers an excellent village beach when the wind is low and the sun is high. Windsurfers can frequently be seen skimming across the harbor when a breeze is blowing, and in late summer a concession offering parasail rides can send you soaring with the seagulls.

It is not by coincidence that most of the buildings in this picturesque village are white. An unwritten law requiring that buildings in the village be painted white or carry no paint at all has survived since Moravian pioneers staked their claim on this harbor in the 19th century.

Fishermen can frequently be found dangling night crawlers off the pier at Anderson Dock. This historic landmark was built in 1860 by Aslag Anderson. The exterior walls of this wooden building are painted with the various names of the boats that have anchored here over the years. This landmark now serves as a public art exhibit hall known as the Francis Hardy Art Gallery and is operated under the control of the Peninsula Arts Association. The Peninsula Art Association was founded in 1937 to promote the arts in Door County.

Other historic sites in Ephraim include the Ephraim Village Hall, the Pioneer Schoolhouse and the Ephraim Moravian Church. (See a walking tour of Ephraim, listed separately.)

The development that has sprung up between Ephraim and Sister Bay in recent years has frustrated many long-time visitors to the Door Peninsula. The increased traffic and start-stop driving can take its toll on the nerves, and travelers wishing to avoid this congestion should plan to avoid this stretch during the peak season.

Sister Bay is the largest community in northern Door County. The village and its surrounding landscape are developing rapidly, but its downtown area maintains its traditional charm. A fine public beach and dock provide excellent access to Green Bay. The village and the bluffs that tower above it take their names from the two publicly owned "sister" islands offshore. These islands are preserved under the jurisdiction of the Wisconsin Natural Areas Preservation Council and provide nesting areas for shorebirds. Birds banded here have reportedly been recaptured from as far away as Panama. The twin "Sister Bluffs" rising above the village reach heights of 130 and 190 feet. Private developments top these bluffs, which provide an excellent view of Green Bay.

Settled in 1857, Sister Bay is best noted for its annual October Fall Fest. This is the largest community celebration in Door County, and thousands visit the village each October to enjoy the crisp autumn air and the colorful changing leaves. During summer, goats can be found grazing on the sod-covered roof of Al Johnson's Swedish Restaurant, creating quite a spectacle.

Departing Sister Bay en route to Ellison Bay, you'll be entering the northern orchard country of the peninsula. A trip east on County Z leads to Rowleys Bay and the mouth of the Mink River Estuary. This Nature Conservancy Preserve is best explored by kayak or canoe, although a walking trail is available off Newport Drive near Newport State Park. The Mink River is one of the most pristine natural areas of the peninsula. Alkaline springs feed this slow-moving river that flows through a vast wetland and past wooded shores before spilling into Lake Michigan at Rowleys Bay.

Continuing on Highway 42 you'll find a sidetrack to Ellison Bluff County Park leading to an impressive vantage point atop bluff headlands overlooking Green Bay. Access to the waters of Green Bay is impossible because of the high limestone precipice separating the wooded parkland from the water. The scenic road leading into the preserve passes an old stone fence before turning to gravel through a cedar forest. An old logging road serves as a nature trail through this 88-acre park.

DOOR COUNTY WINE MAKING

Wine making in Door County began as early as 1862. Today the Door Peninsula Winery produces apple and cherry wine in a schoolhouse built in 1868 in Carlsville, north of Sturgeon Bay. The winery offers guided tours from spring through fall.

Continuing on Highway 42 you'll reach the awesome bluff showcasing Ellison Bay. This bluff was once farmland, but pressure to exploit the outstanding view became intense and a resort now sits upon the overlook. Resort developers, however, took care to maintain the scenic approach, and motorists will not be disappointed as Ellison Bay unfolds before them.

Named for pioneer John Ellison, Ellison Bay was settled in the 1860s. Descending the hill you'll find the Ellison Bay Women's Park on the bayshore. A sand beach and picnic tables provide swimming and picnicking opportunities to the public. The Ellison Bay dock is home to many commercial and charter fishing operations. Passing through the heart of the village you'll find the turn-of-the-century Pioneer Store worthy of a visit.

Ellison Bay has become famous for popularizing the fish boil dinner, a tradition dating back to pioneer days. Fishermen and lumbermen settling the peninsula found an abundance of whitefish and trout in the surrounding waters. By adding potatoes and onions in a large pot, they created a simple and tasty one-kettle dinner. Today modern fish boils utilize basically the same recipe but add a few theatrics to interest spectators, including the "overboil." This is accomplished by adding a large amount of fuel to the outdoor fire just as the fish completes cooking. As flames shoot through the air the water boils over the large kettle, creating a spectacular sight. A cherry pie dessert completes the meal, reminding visitors that this peninsula is still considered "cherryland."

En route to the tip of the peninsula, travelers will enjoy turning left at Gus Klenke's garage on Garrett Bay on the outskirts of Ellison Bay. Gus Klenke is no longer alive, but his service station has become something of a local landmark. Comparisons to the fictitious town of Mayberry become apparent.

Just two blocks from Highway 42 stands The Clearing. This private school for contemplation and study was founded by famed landscape architect Jens Jenson in 1935. Jenson developed The Clearing as a "school of the soil" in the belief that man must return

FISH BOIL TRADITION

Fish boils have long been a part of the Scandinavian heritage in Door County. But the cooking of fish in kettles with potatoes and onions actually originated in lumber camps as an easy way of preparing the fish.

to the soil and learn from nature if he is to find himself. Today the 120-acre grounds he nurtured maintains its enduring appeal. The Clearing is open weekend afternoons from mid-May through October.

A brief sidetrack off Garrett Bay Road leads to Door Bluff Headlands County Park. At over 150 acres, Door Bluff Headlands is the largest county park on the peninsula. The park preserves the woodlots surrounding 200-foot-high Door Bluff, but due to its rugged nature and challenging hikes it is rarely visited. Proceeding on Garrett Bay Road you'll drive along Hedgehog Harbor, so named because hedgehogs, commonly called porcupines, chewed through a boat left to winter on the shores of Green Bay by a pioneer fisherman. Winding along the shore into sleepy Gills Rock, you'll again join Highway 42.

If time is tight and you're anxious to catch the Washington Island car ferry, you'll be heading directly out of Ellison Bay on Highway 42. This road threads northeast past cherry and apple orchards along the scenic countryside to Gills Rock. En route you'll pass the access road to Newport State Park.

Newport is a wilderness park preserving over 2,200 acres of undeveloped forest and shoreline. Its wonderful sand beach provides excellent swimming opportunities, and backpack camping is available. Just before you reach Newport on Newport Lane, you'll pass a wooden marker identifying the Schoenbrun Nature Conservancy. This one-mile-long trail provides walk-in access to the Mink River, a preserved freshwater estuary harboring endangered plants, wildlife and waterfowl.

Just before you make the final turn into Newport State Park, you'll encounter a gravel road leading to Europe Bay Town Park. This little park is sandwiched on both sides by Newport State Park and provides access to Europe Beach, perhaps the finest stretch of sand on the peninsula. If you're heading to the Northport Pier, you can continue down Timberline Road to join Highway 42 south of the dock or backtrack to the highway. Timberline Road is one of those quaint country roads that remind you why the Door Peninsula is such a special place.

STATE PARKS

Peninsula State Park

The entrance is near the village of Fish Creek off Highway 42, 25 miles north of Sturgeon Bay. Address: P.O. Box 218, Fish Creek, WI 54212. Phone: 414-868-3258.

FACILITIES:
There are four campgrounds with a total of 473 campsites. About 72% of these are reservable by mail using the proper DNR form. Reservations are almost mandatory during the summer, and are recommended on autumn weekends. The restrooms are modern and showers are available. A camping fee is charged; non-residents pay more than Wisconsin residents. Also, the fees are higher during the months when the flush toilets are open. There is electricity at 96 sites for an additional charge. The park is open year-round, but with reduced facilities in the off-season. A vehicle admission sticker is required if you park, but is not required to drive through the park. The park covers 3,763 acres.

RECREATION:

The park offers hiking trails, a bicycle trail, tennis courts, a golf course, a swimming beach, ski trails, canoeing and kayaking, an observation tower, a nature center with interpretive programs, an exercise course, a tobogganing slope, and a launch facility for fishing and boating.

With its stunning sunsets, beautiful bays, craggy cliffs and towering trees, it's no wonder that Peninsula State Park is Door County's number-one attraction and the most popular state park in Wisconsin.

Peninsula State Park is located between Fish Creek and Ephraim about 70 miles north of Green Bay via Highways 57 and 42. A welcoming center greets visitors at the Fish Creek entrance. A vehicle admission sticker is required if you stop in the park even just to admire the view or climb the tower.

This is truly a four-season park. Summers in the park bring hordes of visitors escaping urban hustle and bustle. Many stake out a claim on the beach,

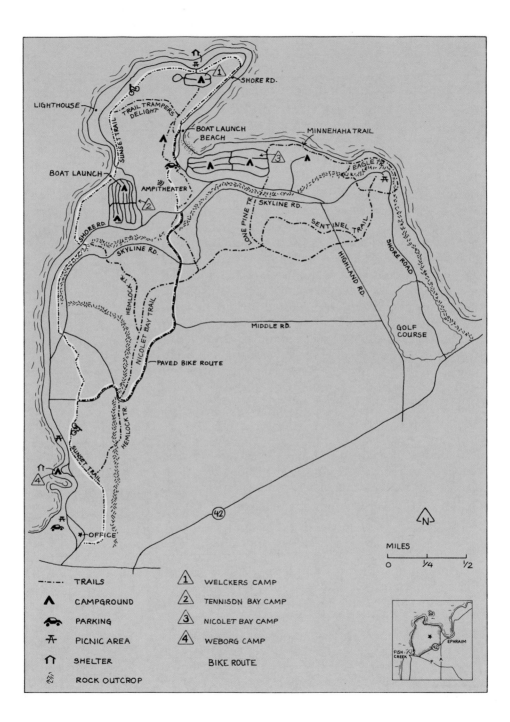

SHORE RD.

LIGHTHOUSE

TRAIL TRAMPERS DELIGHT

BOAT LAUNCH BEACH

MINNEHAHA TRAIL

SUNSET TRAIL

BOAT LAUNCH

AMPITHEATER

EAGLE TR.

LONE PINE TR.

SKYLINE RD.

SENTINEL TRAIL

SHORE RD.

SKYLINE RD.

HEMLOCK TR.

NICOLET BAY TRAIL

HIGHLAND RD.

SHORE ROAD

MIDDLE RD.

GOLF COURSE

PAVED BIKE ROUTE

HEMLOCK TR.

SUNSET TRAIL

OFFICE

42

N

MILES

0   ¼   ½

TRAILS

CAMPGROUND

PARKING

PICNIC AREA

SHELTER

ROCK OUTCROP

1 WELCKERS CAMP

2 TENNISON BAY CAMP

3 NICOLET BAY CAMP

4 WEBORG CAMP

BIKE ROUTE

EPHRAIM

FISH CREEK

42

some pedal through the park along roads that seem tailor-made for a country ride, and others paddle along the shore seeking solitude and seclusion.

Summer is also the season of education and entertainment in the park. Don't leave without taking in a performance by the University of Wisconsin Heritage Ensemble, presented from late June through Labor Day. These family-oriented musical productions feature a lively mixture of history and folklore well worth the small admission charge. You'll also want to consider the variety of programs conducted by the park naturalist during the summer months. These programs are aimed at increasing your knowledge of the natural world here with trees and cliffs forming the walls of your classroom.

A summer hike through the hemlocks will certainly renew your spirit, and a saunter through the pines will have you wishing you could bottle the aroma. Those with a bent toward exercise should not miss the Vita Course. This one-mile exercise circuit asks you to perform various tasks geared toward increasing your strength and improving your balance and coordination. It begins near Nicolet Beach.

An 18-hole golf course, considered by many the most scenic in mid-America, greets visitors at the park's Ephraim entrance. Getting a tee time can be difficult, so reserve one by mail prior to your visit. A tennis court is also in the park, but plan on arriving early if you wish to play.

Fishing is popular along the park shore where anglers search for coho, chinook salmon, rainbow, brown and lake trout, perch, bass and northern pike.

Paddlers will want to visit Horseshoe (Eagle) Island. This 38-acre island is visible from Nicolet Bay and provides hiking and picnicking opportunities.

Autumn travelers are greeted by a kaleidoscope of fall colors, and on October weekends the park can be just as busy as in mid-summer. Many find this time of year the best for hiking. The trails are never crowded, the temperature is brisk and animals are active, increasing your chances to spot wildlife.

Winter finds a handful of hardy tent campers nestled in goose-down sleeping bags dreaming of hot

(opposite page)
PENINSULA STATE PARK

WEBORG MARSH

Weborg Marsh is a ten-acre spring-fed marsh along Shore Road. This area has abundant aquatic vegetation.

spiced wine. Cross-country skiers will find 19 miles of family-oriented ski trails geared to a wide variety of skill levels. If you enjoy snowshoeing, the park can accommodate you on one trail or you may break your own ground elsewhere in the park. The hill on the 17th fairway of the golf course has been set aside for tobogganing and sledding and remains off-limits to snowmobiles.

Indian cultures, most recently the Menomonee, Fox, Winnebago and Iroquois, roamed the woods of Peninsula State Park long before white settlements replaced their simple lifestyle. There is one known Indian encampment site within the park, but there is little doubt this area was heavily used by Native Americans.

It is widely suspected that Jean Nicolet, the first white man to visit the present state of Wisconsin, paid a visit to Nicolet Bay. This was to be a working vacation, however, since Nicolet had hopes of negotiating a treaty with Winnebago Indians. In the narrative of this journey, Nicolet says he stopped for a week at a place two days' journey from the Winnebago village. The principal Winnebago Indian village was at Red Banks, marked by a statue off Highway 57 north of Green Bay. Since it takes just two days to canoe from Red Banks to Nicolet Bay, it is indeed possible that Jean Nicolet was the first tourist on the peninsula.

Today little remains of this Native American presence. A totem pole on the park golf course, however, does mark the grave of Potawatomi Chief Simon Onanquisse Kahquados. Chief Kahquados was laid to rest here on May 30, 1931, before a crowd of some 10,000 spectators, a testimony to his popularity. Admired by both Indians and white people alike, Chief Kahquados was the last of a long line of Potawatomi chiefs who for centuries ruled over the woods, wetlands and wildlife of the Door Peninsula.

In 1842, Increase Claflin was the first white settler to homestead in what was to become Peninsula State Park. In the early 1850s, Evan Nelson and Peter Weborg led some 35 families in settling a stretch of shore now called Weborg Point. Finding the soil poor for

PENINSULA PARK GOLF
Development of the park golf course began shortly after the park was established in 1910. It was begun by a group of Ephraim businessmen as a nine-hole course with sand "greens." Later the course was expanded to its current 18 holes.

(opposite page)

The scenic views from the back nine of the Peninsula State Park championship golf course are unbeatable.

farming, these settlers soon turned to the surrounding waters where abundant whitefish and herring populations fed their families. As fishing began to decline, these pioneers turned their efforts to lumber production, depending on the market created by steamships plying Green Bay waters. Eagle Lighthouse, established in 1868, helped guide these ships safely to dock at Eagle (Horseshoe) Island where they could take on firewood. By the early 1900s, steamships were making weekly visits to Fish Creek and Ephraim. But the forests were not limitless, and hopes to establish an agricultural base were not abandoned. In 1866, the first cherry and apple orchards were established on the peninsula. The cool, damp influence of Lake Michigan proved to be ideal for the growth of these trees, and fruit production remains an important aspect of the local economy. Today, a tribute to Door County's first farmer, Ole Olson, can be found in the Nicolet Bay Campground. Campers driving a tent stake through this shallow soil may suspect Ole died a hungry man.

If you're a car camper, you've come to the right place. Peninsula State Park offers the most complete public camping facilities in Door County. The park has four campgrounds: Nicolet Bay, Welcker's, Tennison Bay and Weborg. There are a total of 473 campsites, 96 with electricity. The campsites range from outstanding to adequate depending on the location. Several sites are located directly on the water, and demand for these sites, particularly in Nicolet Bay, always exceeds the number available. Make camping reservations early.

Campsite reservations must be postmarked no earlier than the first working day of the new year. Reservations postmarked earlier will be returned. Reservations for a two-day minimum (three days on holiday weekends) are accepted for the period starting May 1 and ending the last weekend in October. Reservations must be made on an official form available from any Wisconsin state park, but photocopies are acceptable. Remember to include the reservation fee. Peninsula receives approximately 3,000 requests for campsites in early January.

CAMPING BARGAINS

Originally, camping was not limited to individual sites but to individual areas within the park. Camping was free at first and later a 50-cent-per-day or $5-per-year fee was charged.

If you arrive at Peninsula State Park on one of the many summer days when the "no vacancy" sign is posted, the park staff will attempt to accommodate you. Ask that your name be added to the waiting list. The waiting list starts after the last campsite is filled. The park staff will also help you to locate a vacancy

NICOLET BAY CAMPGROUND

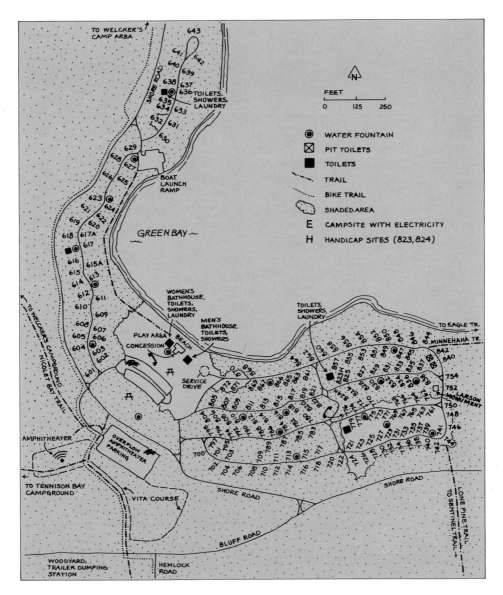

TENNISON BAY CAMPGROUND

at one of the many private campgrounds in the area. The following day at 10 a.m., all those campers already with a campsite wishing to transfer to another campsite or extend their stay must meet at the park visitor station, and the campground shuffle begins. Campsites are reassigned and camping permits are extended as space permits.

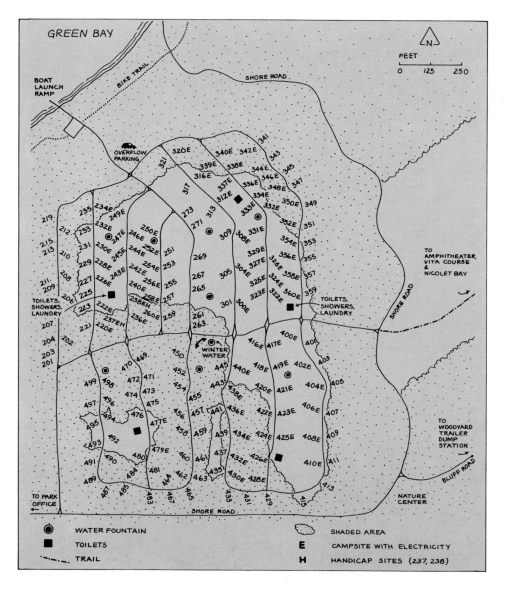

At 11 a.m. campers wishing to secure a campsite must meet at the visitor station, and the park staff fills vacant campsites using the waiting list to establish preference. You must be present each day to remain on the waiting list even if you are unsuccessful in acquiring a campsite. The procedure continues each day until you get a campsite or your vacation expires. The process is admittedly tiresome but it does assure some semblance of equity in campsite assignments.

NICOLET BAY CAMPGROUND: Nicolet Bay is the largest and often the busiest of the park's four campgrounds. Situated on Nicolet Bay, this campground affords waterfront campsites, easy access to the beach and glowing sunsets. The campground is divided into two sections, separated by the Nicolet Bay Day Use Area. The northern section of the campground has 45 sites while the southern portion has 146 units. Much of the campground is nicely wooded, except for the southeast one-quarter which is open field.

This campground, like the others at Peninsula State Park, has modern showers and facilities. Showers are also available at the Nicolet Bay Beach. The waterfront campsites on Nicolet Bay are in very high demand. Consider yourself lucky if you secure one, then sit back and enjoy the view—it's one of the best on the peninsula.

TENNISON BAY CAMPGROUND: Tennison Bay is an appealing family oriented campground with 189 sites. It is the only campground that is open year-round with winter water supplies. The campground has both shaded and open campsites, with those located in the spruce plantation particularly desirable. Boaters enjoy camping here because one of two park ramps is located in the campground. A play area greets children eager to burn some calories after a long car ride. All campsites in Tennison Bay are reservable from May through October. The nature center, amphitheater and Nicolet Bay beach are all a leisurely stroll away.

WELCKER'S CAMPGROUND: Welcker's Point is the site of an 81-unit campground noted for its heavily wooded campsites. There are six sites with electric

GAME FARM
During the 1920s and 1930s, Peninsula State Park was the location of the state's first game farm. The farm and rearing pens were located near the present group camping area and the open area of Nicolet Bay campground.

CCC CONSTRUCTION
During the depression years, a Civilian Conservation Corps camp was established at the park. CCC men built towers, stone fences, hiking trails and many of the stone buildings found in the park today.

hookups in the campground. Campers pitching their tents here have easy access to the sunset bicycle trail, and it's only a short ride to the park beach. A shelter building adjacent to the campground on the bay shore provides a dry haven for campers caught in a sudden downpour. Wildlife in the park is abundant and there is an excellent chance of spotting white-tail deer right outside of this campground.

WEBORG CAMPGROUND: Weborg Campground has only 13 campsites. Even though many of the sites are unshaded, the campground is extremely popular because of its unique location. The waters of Green Bay border this triangular-shaped campground on two sides. All of the sites here are electric except 112. There is a possibility sites 103 and 104 may be eliminated to accommodate the park's sewer system, so

WELCKER'S CAMPGROUND

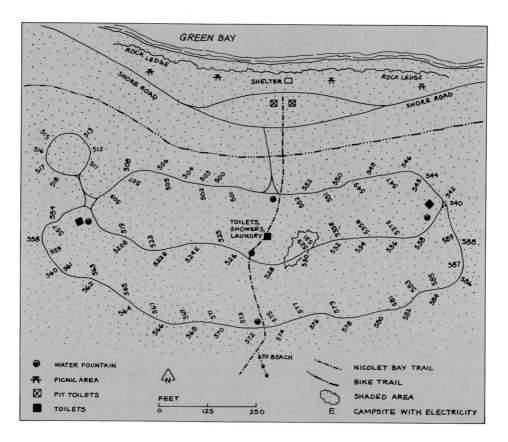

GREEN BAY

ROCK LEDGE

SHORE ROAD

SHELTER

ROCK LEDGE

SHORE ROAD

TOILETS, SHOWERS, LAUNDRY

TO BEACH

●	WATER FOUNTAIN
禾	PICNIC AREA
⊠	PIT TOILETS
■	TOILETS

NICOLET BAY TRAIL
BIKE TRAIL
SHADED AREA
E   CAMPSITE WITH ELECTRICITY

N

FEET
0   125   250

WEBORG CAMPGROUND

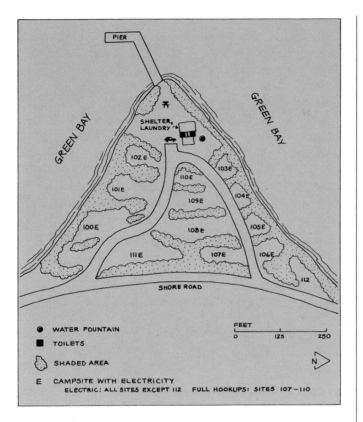

- ● WATER FOUNTAIN
- ■ TOILETS
- SHADED AREA
- E CAMPSITE WITH ELECTRICITY
  ELECTRIC: ALL SITES EXCEPT 112   FULL HOOKUPS: SITES 107-110

CEDAR-SPRUCE SWAMP

A cedar-spruce swamp is one of two scientific areas within the park. This 53-acre forest contains a white cedar-spruce forest on an abandoned Lake Michigan beach. Also present is a population of dwarf lake iris, a threatened species in Wisconsin.

check before attempting to reserve these sites. A major attraction for those either staying here or visiting from other campgrounds in the park is the large concrete dock adjacent to the campground. The dock provides fishing opportunities and a scenic view of Fish Creek just across the bay.

HIKING TRAILS

The Vita Course: This one-mile exercise circuit begins across from Nicolet Bay Beach near the overflow parking area. Eleven exercise stations instruct the user to perform various exercises designed to promote strength, stamina and coordination. Participants can walk or jog the course, pausing at each wooden station for exercise instructions. This is a great way to escape Nicolet Bay Beach for a quick romp through the forest.

BEECH-MAPLE FOREST

The 80-acre beech-maple forest within the park has been designated a State Scientific Area. This forest includes American beech, sugar maple, hemlock, red oak, white cedar and white birch.

(opposite page)

Lake effect snow and groomed ski trails combine to offer outstanding cross country skiing on the county's lakeshore.

Eagle Trail: The steep and rocky Eagle Trail (two miles) traverses some of the highest bluffs on the Door Peninsula. Budget 1.5 hours for this hike and pick up the trail head at either Eagle Panorama, just west of Eagle Tower on Shore Road, or at Eagle Tower. Several springs, including Eagle Spring, can be found on this awe-inspiring hike.

Hemlock Trail: A wonderful aroma drifts through the air as hikers saunter through the cedars on the 1.8-mile Hemlock Trail. Be prepared to return via the same route, or pick up the Sunset bike trail for an alternate return on this one- to two-hour hike. The trail head can be reached off Shore Road just south of Tennison Bay Campground.

Lone Pine Trail: Beginning at the southeast corner of Nicolet Bay Campground, the Lone Pine Trail climbs the limestone bluff that forms the backbone of Peninsula State Park. Passing the remains of the solitary white pine tree the trail is named for, hikers have the option of returning to camp or continuing down the Sentinel or Nicolet Bay trails.

Minihaha Trail: This short trail (.7 miles) along the lakeshore connects the Nicolet Bay Campground with the Eagle Trail. Pick up the trail near Nicolet Bay Campground site number 844.

Sentinel Trail: The popular Sentinel Trail loop (two miles) begins at Eagle Tower and winds through a maple, beech and red pine forest. Quiet hikers may see deer in the meadows on this hike. Budget 1.5 hours since the terrain is gentle, and pick up the half-mile connecting trail that leads to the Lone Pine and Nicolet Bay trails if you're up for more exercise.

Trail Trampers Delight: The short Trail Trampers Delight (.75 miles) traces its name to the early 1920s, when hikers walked from Nicolet Bay to Eagle Lighthouse. The heavily wooded trail provided escape from the summer sun, which made it a trail tramper's "delight." The trail head can be picked up at the historic Eagle Lighthouse off Shore Road. The trail ends at Nicolet Bay Campground.

CROSS-COUNTRY SKI TRAILS

Peninsula State Park reminds one of a postcard of Norway when five inches of fresh powder are weighing down the limbs of lofty pine trees along the cross-country ski trails. Breathtaking views, deep forests

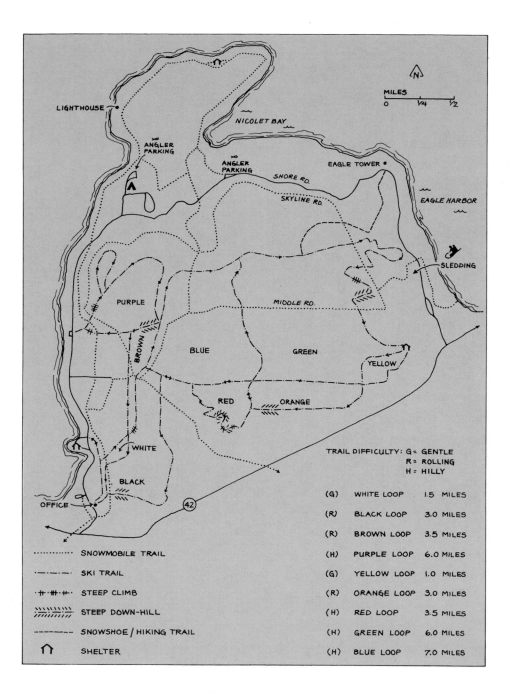

MILES

N

LIGHTHOUSE

ANGLER PARKING

NICOLET BAY

ANGLER PARKING

SHORE RD.

EAGLE TOWER

SKYLINE RD.

EAGLE HARBOR

SLEDDING

PURPLE

MIDDLE RD.

BROWN

BLUE

GREEN

YELLOW

WHITE

RED

ORANGE

BLACK

OFFICE

42

TRAIL DIFFICULTY: G = GENTLE
R = ROLLING
H = HILLY

.... SNOWMOBILE TRAIL

–·–·–· SKI TRAIL

·+·+·+· STEEP CLIMB

STEEP DOWN-HILL

– – – – SNOWSHOE / HIKING TRAIL

⌂ SHELTER

(G)	WHITE LOOP	1.5 MILES
(R)	BLACK LOOP	3.0 MILES
(R)	BROWN LOOP	3.5 MILES
(H)	PURPLE LOOP	6.0 MILES
(G)	YELLOW LOOP	1.0 MILES
(R)	ORANGE LOOP	3.0 MILES
(H)	RED LOOP	3.5 MILES
(H)	GREEN LOOP	6.0 MILES
(H)	BLUE LOOP	7.0 MILES

and snow-covered meadows beckon skiers to explore this picturesque winter playground. The variety of the ski trails is what keeps people coming back. The most challenging cross-country hills on the peninsula are found on the purple loop, while beginners will find both the white and yellow trails mellow and scenic.

You'll generally find snow here from January through March, but a phone call (414-868-3258) can give you up-to-date conditions. A Wisconsin state park admission sticker is required to park in the ski lots and winter camping is available for the (very) warm-blooded.

Skiers wishing to avoid encounters with snowmobiles will be interested to note Peninsula has a quiet zone encompassing portions of the blue, green, red and orange loops where snowmobiles are prohibited.

Park rangers groom 19 miles of ski trails, and most of these are one-way except short portions of the red, orange, and blue loops as indicated on the map.

Skiers have four parking lots from which to begin their trips. Lots 1, 2 and 3 are accessible from the park's Fish Creek entrance. Lot 4 is reached by turning left off Highway 42 north of Fish Creek on County A. Lot 3, reached off Shore Road, caters to those wishing to ski the advanced loop. Warming shelters at parking lots 2 and 4 are open winter weekends. The ski trails intersect so it is possible to return to the wrong parking lot while completing your planned loop. Plan carefully.

The one-mile **yellow trail** is the park's easiest loop. Beginners will find a forgiving double-tracked trail traversing very gentle terrain through hardwood forests and old fields.

The **white trail** is another beginner's trail that's just a touch more difficult (1.5 miles) than the yellow trail.

Skiers with some experience will enjoy cruising down several challenging hills on the three-mile orange trail. There's nothing here too difficult for the intermediate skier.

The **black trail**, also three miles, is geared toward the intermediate skier as well. This loop takes skiers through relatively remote areas of the park over

(opposite page)
PENINSULA WINTER TRAILS

EAGLE LIGHTHOUSE

Eagle Lighthouse was established in 1868. Today, the light is automated. Tours are conducted during the summer months by the Door County Historical Society, whose members have restored the structure to its 1890s condition. An admission fee is charged.

gently rolling terrain. Expect a tough uphill climb where the black and brown trails separate from the white loop. Watch out for the steep curving hill on the last half-mile section.

The 3.5-mile **brown trail** is another intermediate loop and shares the steep uphill climb encountered on the black loop where these trails separate from the white trail. The payback is a challenging downhill stretch where the trail merges with the purple loop.

The **green trail** is a beautiful loop for an intermediate skier willing to travel six miles. Skiers venture through remote areas of the park, encountering a variety of forest and field. You'll find challenging hills between Highland and Middle roads, so be forewarned.

Fast downhills and plenty of climbing characterize a half mile of the red loop, but the other three miles are relatively flat.

The **blue loop** is a great trail. The seven miles hit all the hills on the red and green loops plus a long section of lesser used trail. There's access to the purple loop if you still have calories to burn.

The exhilarating, challenging **purple trail** (six miles) is groomed to provide skate skiing opportunities for those so inclined. Hills are abundant and not for the faint of heart. Sven's Panorama is a "must see." This loop is not recommended for inexperienced skiers. Those wishing to hit the hills quickly have direct access from parking lot 3.

TOWN, VILLAGE AND COUNTY PARKS

Frank E. Murphy County Park *(14 acres)*

Located off County B just south of Egg Harbor you'll find an excellent sand beach, a concrete fishing pier and boat launching facilities to access Horseshoe Bay. This popular county park is named after Frank E. Murphy, a wealthy Green Bay businessman and prominent civic leader.

Across from the park is Horseshoe Bay Farms. Built in 1917, no expense was spared to construct the handsome barns located at the intersection of County B and G. These barns once housed Murphy's nationally famous black-and-white Holstein herd.

Murphy is the most popular county park in the Door County Park system. Still, the beach is rarely crowded and the dock is seldom busy. Recent improvements to the pier have provided excellent fishing opportunities for anglers, and expanded boat launching facilities have made this a popular access point for boaters. A volleyball court, playground and picnic tables make this an excellent site for a family picnic.

Harbor View Village Park *(.37 acres)*

This small landscaped park in the Village of Egg Harbor has a few benches and a flagpole. It provides a scenic view of the Harbor and the village dock from Highway 42.

Egg Harbor Village Park *(1.75 acres)*

The Egg Harbor Village Park marks the center of shoreside activity in this picturesque community. The village dock provides 43 boat slips, but all but four are rented on a seasonal basis. There is a two-lane boat launching ramp, and ample parking for both cars and trailers. Picnic tables and grills provide picnicking opportunities, and this is a great place to begin a bayshore bike ride.

HORSESHOE BAY FARMS

The Horseshoe Bay barns located across from Frank E. Murphy County Park were built in 1917. Some historians believe they mark the end of the pioneer building era in Door County since they were constructed using relatively modern techniques.

Fish Creek Community Center Park

(1.5 acres)

The Fish Creek Community Center on Highway 42 houses the Town of Gibraltar library and serves as a meeting place for local government. There are a pair of tennis courts next to the library, but parking is limited, so you may wish to secure a parking place on Highway 42.

Sunset Town Park *(1.19 acres)*

This park is aptly named since it provides an excellent place to watch the sun go down over the bay. A footpath leads through a scenic wooded grove from the Fish Creek business section to this small park. You'll have a great view of Chambers Island from the park benches, but there is no parking available.

Fish Creek Town Park *(.25 acres)*

The Fish Creek Town Park and its adjacent dock is the center of activity during the various festivals that the village celebrates. A low stone wall along the bayshore surrounds the property, making swimming difficult. The adjacent town-owned dock accommodates about 30 boats. Fishermen are often found dangling bait or casting off the dock. Perch is the most popular target, but anglers also land an occasional trout, salmon or northern pike.

Chambers Island Lighthouse Town Park

(40 acres)

This Gibraltar town park offers visitors the only public access to Chambers Island and its wonderful beach. The dilapidated pier is no longer useful since it is not attached to shore. Boaters docking here will have to throw out an anchor and wade or take a dinghy to the beach. Surprisingly, there is a public access road running through the park, but vehicles are few on this isolated island. The lighthouse on the island is of historical significance.

Anderson Dock *(.25 acres)*

Often the most luxurious yachts plying the peninsula are found docking at the twelve boat slips provided at Ephraim's Anderson Dock. The adjacent historic warehouse is now the site of the Hardy Memorial Art Gallery and the Anderson Store Museum.

Eagle Harbor offers an interesting insight into the seafaring past of this quaint village. It's also a convenient place to try fishing. Bass and perch are often caught right off the dock. An historic plaque placed by the Ephraim Foundation indicates the historical significance of this site. Parking is available.

Sister Bay Village Park *(2 acres)*

A guarded swimming beach and concrete pier complement the Sister Bay central business district at this village park. Located on Highway 42 (Bay Shore Drive), this public park and beach also offers a picnic shelter, swings and picnic tables. Parking is available for about 20 cars. It's best to arrive early in the day to avoid congestion.

Ellison Bluff County Park *(88 acres)*

Located off Highway 42 between the villages of Sister Bay and Ellison Bay, Ellison Bluff County Park sits upon wooded headlands. A stairway leads to a viewing site providing an awe-inspiring view of Green Bay waters. Access to Green Bay waters is all but impossible since a high limestone precipice separates the viewing site from the shore. There are picnic facilities and parking for about 15 cars.

Gateway Village Park *(1.62 acres)*

A tourist information cabin at the intersection of State Highways 42 and 57 stands as the gateway to Sister Bay. The cabin was constructed in 1866 and was restored in 1976 as a bicentennial restoration project. This is a convenient location to stretch your legs and plan your visit to Sister Bay.

Ephraim Village Playground *(2.7 acres)*

The Ephraim Village Playground is tucked away off County Q on a bluff above the downtown district. A basketball court, three tennis courts and playground equipment mark the location. This park is next to the grammar school and there is boat trailer parking available.

Sister Bay Athletic Field *(6 acres)*

Door County residents love watching their summer league baseball teams battle it out, and the Sister Bay Athletic Field is one of the locations where these matches take place. Located on North Highland Road, the field has bleacher stands to provide you with a place to sit while you enjoy a little summer baseball— Door County-style.

Ellison Bay Women's Club Park *(3 acres)*

This park, also known as the Ellison Bay Community Center, has two swimming beaches separated by a dock. One of these two secluded beaches is sand and offers a great place to take a dip. The park also has two tennis courts, playground equipment, a meeting house, and a pleasant lawn for relaxing. Parking is available on nearby streets.

Ellison Bay Men's Club Park *(.6 acres)*

This park is also known as Ellison Bay Town Park and offers two boat ramps, a 24-slip boat dock and considerable parking. It is centrally located off Highway 42.

(opposite page)

During the summer, Ephraim's historic Anderson Dock, serves as home to the Francis Hardy Art Gallery. The warehouse walls bear the art deco inscriptions of vessels which once lay anchor here.

PRESERVES

Fuller Tract Natural Area

This preserve, also known as the Peninsula Center Sanctuary, is a 160-acre natural area located off County E, west of Egg Harbor. Two small stone monuments mark the eastern boundary of the property. Parking for one or two cars is available off the unmarked dirt road that parallels the northern border of the property.

FACILITIES:
A day-use area, this preserve is open year-round to explorers on foot or skis.

RECREATION:
Bird-watching, hiking, cross-country skiing.

An impressive stone fence reveals countless hours of laborious toil upon the abandoned farm fields of the Fuller Tract. Nature is reclaiming this land, just as Judson Fuller wished it would when he deeded the property to the University of Wisconsin in 1970. Fuller, a UW alumnus from River Forest, Illinois, put no restrictions on the property, but did request that it be left intact "as an outdoor nature laboratory for university students of botany, wildlife and ecology." To date, Fuller's wishes have been respected, and red pine, cedar, birch and maple trees are again gaining a hold in the rocky soil.

Also known as the Peninsula Center Sanctuary, naturalists from the nearby Ridges Sanctuary occasionally offer summer birding expeditions to this parcel, providing an excellent opportunity for further discovery.

There is a sad footnote in the history of the Fuller Tract. A few days after the Fullers deeded the property to the University of Wisconsin Foundation, on December 18, 1970, they suffered a tragic auto accident. Judson Fuller's wife, Jessie, was killed and Mr. Fuller was critically injured. Today the Peninsula Center Sanctuary serves as a living memorial to Jessie Fuller and those who tilled the soil before her.

BEACHES

Horseshoe Bay (Frank E. Murphy) Beach

This park is on Horseshoe Bay, 2.5 miles south of Egg Harbor. Take County G down the shoreline to County B. You'll find a great swimming beach, a concrete pier, and an excellent view of Horseshoe Bay. There are picnic facilities and a boat ramp as well. The park is about 14 acres in size.

Egg Harbor Village Beach

A stone wall runs along the shore of this pebble beach. While the beach isn't sand, it does provide a nice view of the harbor and the village. Playground equipment can be found along the grass lawn, and an access road runs through the park grounds to private homes along the northern boundary. A resort forms the southern boundary. Across from the beach on County G a recently acquired 10-acre woodlot protects bedrock outcrops, glacial dune ridges and a small wetland.

Chambers Island Beach

You'll need a boat to reach the beach on Chambers Island but it's certainly worth the effort. Deep sand and lovely water will surround you at this 40-acre Town of Gibraltar preserve. Located on the northern shore of the island, this park is a popular spot for boaters to toss out an anchor. The lack of adequate docking facilities will require that you row, paddle or wade to shore. An airport runway is found behind the beach.

Ephraim Public Beach

The comfortable sand bottom of Eagle Harbor welcomes the tender feet of swimmers taking a dip at the Ephraim village beach. Several years ago, when

Lake Michigan was undergoing a period of high water, this beach all but disappeared. Now that Lake Michigan has retreated the exposed beach is a great place to stretch out a blanket and enjoy the cliffs of Peninsula State Park, visible across Eagle Harbor.

Fish Creek Village Beach

A marked swimming area, easy access and a commanding view of Peninsula State Park combine to draw hundreds of sun lovers to the Fish Creek Public Beach each summer. Drawn by swing sets and a shal-

The best body surfing waves on the penin-sula are found at Whitefish Dunes State Park south of Jackson-port.

92

low bay, this beach is a favorite destination of families vacationing on the peninsula. The shallow water here is often several degrees warmer than on the lake-shore, and brave youngsters can be found swimming here all summer long. The only way to beat the crowds is to arrive at dusk when the last traces of daylight flee across the moored sailboats and even the hardiest beachgoers retire.

Nicolet Bay Beach

Nicolet Bay Beach is often crowded, but that's because it's one of the best beaches on the peninsula. The beach commands a stunning view of Nicolet Bay and Horseshoe Island. The water here is often warmer than elsewhere on the bay side because the shallow water absorbs the sun's heat and holds it. This is also a central meeting spot for boaters on the peninsula, and the grounds behind the beach have been the site of many frisbee, football and volleyball games. Parents will find play equipment for their children, and sailboats, canoes and sailboards may be rented during the summer. The swimming area is well marked. Once at Peninsula State Park, follow Shore Road from the park's Fish Creek entrance—you can't miss it.

Sister Bay Village Beach

Sister Bay offers one of the few guarded beaches on the Door Peninsula. The nearby dock and pleasant surroundings bring a bustle of activity to this beach during summer.

Ellison Bay Women's Park Beach

This small beach is rarely crowded and the surrounding grounds provide excellent picnicking opportunities. A dock separates the pebble beach from the sand beach. Tennis courts are found nearby.

BICYCLE TOURS

Egg Harbor–Heartland Tour

This tour begins along a bayshore cliff before winding through the Door County heartland to Kangaroo Lake, where swimming is available, before the return to Egg Harbor.

Begin this trek at the village dock in Egg Harbor and follow the bayshore up White Cliff Road. Parts of this ride traverse terrain that is moderate to steep, but the views from the bluffs are worth the effort. So, climb the cliff and cross Highway 42. You're now on Juddville Road. Take Juddville Road to County A. Turn right on A. This takes you past the farms and fields of northern Door County. Continue on A as it crosses County EE and County E until you reach Wooded Lane. Cross Wooded Lane and take the next left on Beach Road. Beach Road dead ends at a public access to Kangaroo Lake. If you're up for a swim, this is a great place to do so. To continue, with the lake

EGG
HARBOR–
HEARTLAND
BICYCLE
TOUR

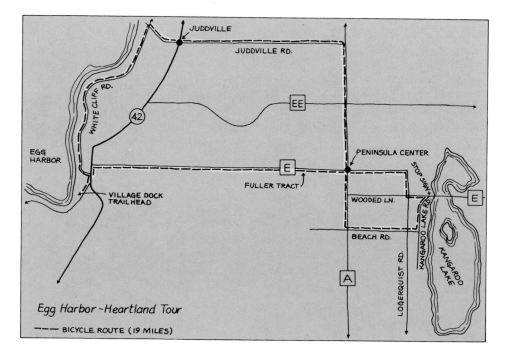

Egg Harbor–Heartland Tour

- - - BICYCLE ROUTE (19 MILES)

94

at your back turn right on the first road from the water. This is Kangaroo Lake Road. Take this road to the stop sign and turn left. Heading up the hill you'll bear right at the sign for Logerquist Road. This road becomes County E. Heading down E you'll find a stone marker commemorating the Fuller Tract Peninsula Sanctuary. Remain on E and you'll intersect with Highway 42 just north of the village limits.

Bicyclists travel the Sunset Bike Trail on a ribbon of limestone scree which winds through the forest and along the bay shore of Peninsula State Park.

95

Sunset Tour *(9 miles)*

The tour winds through Peninsula State Park on the Sunset Bike Trail, providing five miles of traffic-free travel over limestone screenings before connecting with paved park roads. The ride begins just south of the park's visitor contact station. A wide-tire mountain bike is ideal for negotiating the gravel trail, but any bicycle will suffice. You'll encounter two-way traffic (bicycles) as you begin this loop so be on the lookout. Soon you'll be crossing a causeway over a beautiful marsh, where waterfowl are often resting, then hugging the bayshore for an outstanding view of Green Bay. If you're up for a swim, pack your suit since the trail takes you near the Nicolet Bay Beach. After arriving at the beach follow the bike trail markers along Shore Road where you'll pass the overflow parking lot and the Vita Course en route to paved Hemlock Road. Follow Hemlock Road to Middle Road and bear right to return to the Sunset Trail. Turn left on the Sunset Trail at the top of the hill after you pass Blossomburg Cemetery, and you'll be heading back to the trail head.

The terrain is moderate, but please note that you'll be sharing the Sunset Trail with other cyclists, wheelchair users and white-tail deer. The tour uses about four miles of roads where you might encounter cars with protruding mirrors. Use prudent speed. (*See map on page 70*)

CANOE AND KAYAK ROUTES

Eagle Harbor Excursion

Eagle Harbor may well be the most beautiful bay on the Door Peninsula. It's no wonder that early Moravians chose this site to build a church and carve their homes from this spectacular setting. Take Highway 42 to Ephraim and put in at the Ephraim public boat landing. Beginners should hug the shoreline where the village provides a picturesque background as you paddle along admiring the beautiful summer homes lining this natural harbor. Directly across the harbor are the limestone cliffs of Peninsula State Park. Experts may wish to paddle across the bay to explore the cliffs and caves. This is a good place to spend an hour or a day, and to cool off there's a public swimming beach south of the boat landing.

Horseshoe Island

To get to the put-in at Peninsula State Park, follow Shore Road to Nicolet Bay Beach. This trip offers wooded undeveloped shoreline, towering cliffs and Lake Michigan islands.

From Nicolet Bay Beach, it's a two-mile paddle to Horseshoe Island. This 38-acre sanctuary was once called Eagle Island, but its natural harbor and unique shape led to the name change. Administered as part of Peninsula State Park, the island serves as a picnic area for paddlers and a protected harbor for sailors. This trip merits an expert rating in an open canoe because once you hit open water beyond Nicolet Bay, swells can develop that aren't recognizable from shore. This trip is best attempted in mid-summer under fair skies and a promising forecast.

The crossing is somewhat less of a challenge for kayakers, and those wishing to continue island hopping can round the point on the western shore of the mainland to the Strawberry Islands. These islands are privately held, but truly a pleasure to behold. Navigation chart: NOAA #14909.

Chambers Island

The put-in for this open water crossing is the Tennison Bay Boat Landing at Peninsula State Park. Follow Shore Road from the Peninsula State Park entrance to Tennison Bay Campground.

The Strawberry Islands, which include Pirate, Jack, Little Strawberry and Adventure islands, provide the only protection between Peninsula State Park and Chambers Island for kayakers planning this ambitious day trip. Chambers Island lies six miles from shore. A former Coast Guard lighthouse station on the northwest corner of the island is now a 40-acre day-use park that includes a small beach with picnic facilities for day paddlers. Sea kayakers en route to Michigan will find this park a convenient resting place during their crossing.

The historic Island Lighthouse retired along with the last lighthouse keeper in 1950. The rest of the island is privately owned. Rumor has it a stolen Fort Howard payroll was buried here many years ago, but so far the only treasure taken from the island has been locked in the memory of kayakers as they paddle back to shore.

This trip is for expert sea kayakers. Navigation chart: NOAA #14909.

CITIES, TOWNS AND VILLAGES

The Village of Egg Harbor *(pop. 230)*

Limestone bluffs rise to protect the natural bay at Egg Harbor from the fierce and often unpredictable storms that occasionally blow over the waters of Green Bay. Perhaps it was this protection that tempted Levi and Jacob Thorp in 1855 to purchase 1,600 acres where the village now stands. After constructing a dock, the pair took up the cordwood business, following in the footsteps of a third brother, Asa Thorp. Asa was already supplying cordwood to ships docking at his pier in Fish Creek.

Business boomed, and as time passed Levi Thorp became one of the wealthiest businessmen north of Sturgeon Bay. The historic "Cupola House" he constructed in 1871 remains the most impressive building in the village.

Tales vary as to how Egg Harbor was christened. One story, related by Elizabeth Fisher Baird, wife of a famous Green Bay attorney, claims the harbor received its name following a playful bout in 1825 during which eggs were used as ammunition in a mock naval battle. Says Baird, "We began to see eggs flying in the air . . . I crawled under the tarpaulin, where I was comparatively safe, although an occasional egg would strike me on the head."

A less colorful version holds that peninsula pioneer Increase Claflin named the harbor after finding a nest of duck eggs on the shore of the bay. Claflin is also credited with naming Fish Creek, Horseshoe Bay, Hat Island, the Strawberry Islands and Eagle (Horseshoe) Island, lending further credence to the origin of the village name.

After reaching a peak population of over 1,000 residents in 1910, Egg Harbor today is primarily a resort community with a sprinkling of orchards and dairy farms in the surrounding countryside. The population swells during the summer months from its winter size of about 230.

One of the geologic wonders of the peninsula can be found just south of the village in a fissure of rock

THE CUPOLA HOUSE

The Cupola House was built in 1871 by Levi Thorp. Today it remains an Egg Harbor landmark and the most striking example of Gothic Revival-style architecture in Door County.

known as Tecumseh Cave. The cave is over 1,750 feet long, the longest cave known in Wisconsin. It was discovered by local hunters in 1879. Located on private property, the cave is open only to qualified individuals with a legitimate scientific interest. The owners and a few members of the Wisconsin Speleologic Society have explored the cave, but to date no one has reached its conclusion. The cave takes its name from the legend surrounding an Indian chief named Tecumseh. It is said that soldiers were pursuing the sly chief when he ducked into the cave. A guard was stationed at the entrance, but Tecumseh never emerged. He was reportedly seen alive and well later on, having eluded his would-be captors. A second entrance to the cave has never been discovered.

Egg Harbor Village Beach: The beach is located at the south end of the village. Exit Highway 42 at County G. The small pebble beach has a great view of Egg Harbor.

Village Dock and Park: This launch site is off Dock Road·in the center of Egg Harbor. Take Highway 42 to Dock Road. In addition to a boat ramp, the two-acre park offers a pier and picnic facilities.

Frank E. Murphy County Park: This park is on Horseshoe Bay, 2.5 miles south of Egg Harbor. Take County G down the shoreline to County B. You'll find a great swimming beach, a concrete pier, and an excellent view of Horseshoe Bay. There are picnic facilities and a boat ramp as well. The park is about 14 acres in size.

Library: The library at Egg Harbor is off Highway 42 in the village. The phone: 414-868-3334.

Birch Creek Music Center: In addition to gorgeous scenery, this is one of the extras Door County offers to enhance its claim as a vacation paradise. During the summer, students from the Birch Creek Music Center perform free concerts in the gazebo of the Cupola House in Egg Harbor. If one of these concerts whets your appetite for more, Birch Creek students perform nearby in a rustic but comfortable barn from late June to mid-August. For reservations write: P.O. Box 230, Egg Harbor, WI 54209, or call: 414-868-3763.

Fourth of July: Another event worth attending is the Fourth of July parade, which finds tourists and locals alike lining the highway as floats pass, marking another summer in Door County.

The Village of Fish Creek *(pop. 250)*

The gentle descent down Highway 42 into the village of Fish Creek brings visitors to the heart of the northern Door Peninsula. Plans by the Wisconsin Department of Transportation in 1987 to dynamite this spectacular bluff in the interest of highway safety were met with such vehement opposition by local residents that modifications were made to preserve the road's scenic integrity.

Increase Claflin was the first white settler to stake a claim in Fish Creek, although Asa Thorp is credited with founding the village. He constructed a dock here and initiated a commercial cordwood enterprise in 1853. What remains of Thorp's cabin still stands near Founder's Square among the shops and galleries that today provide the center of commerce in the village.

The creek itself was once a rich spawning area for fish. But when timber was stripped from its banks, erosion took its toll and the once-navigable stream today is barely deep enough for a canoe. Strides are being made to protect the stream, however. Recently, the state of Wisconsin purchased a portion of the stream bank, adding the acreage to Peninsula State Park.

Visitors with an hour to spare should not miss the scenic drive down Cottage Row. Here are some of the most exclusive summer "cottages" on the peninsula. It's fun to imagine owning one of these regal retreats, but the view from your tent on the shores of Peninsula State Park's Nicolet Bay is even better than theirs.

Fish Creek, with a permanent population of about 250, offers a library and a civic association to aid people in the area. The library, off Highway 42, offers tourist information as well as library services. The phone: 414-868-3471. The address of the civic association: Box 1974, Fish Creek, WI 54212.

FOUNDER'S SQUARE

In the heart of Fish Creek, the complex of shops, restaurants and galleries is known collectively as "Founder's Square." The buildings were originally part of a summer hotel and cottage resort operated by Edgar Thorp.

A squall rolls into Fish Creek.

A number of "must see" cultural events await summer visitors to this village. Of particular note are performances by the Peninsula Players at the "Theatre in a Garden," classical music performances during the Peninsula Music Festival, and the Heritage Ensemble performances held in the amphitheater of Peninsula State Park.

The Peninsula Players: Touted as the world's oldest professional resident summer theater, the players perform in a peaceful open-air bay shore setting with a relaxed rural atmosphere. In 1985 they celebrated their 50th anniversary. For information or reservations phone: 414-868-3287.

The Peninsula Music Festival: The Peninsula Music Festival has brought top-caliber classical musicians to Fish Creek for several weeks each August since 1953. Sponsored by the Peninsula Arts Association, the festival is the highlight of the summer for those combining a love of classical music with their love of the Door Peninsula. For information write: P.O. Box 71, Sister Bay, WI 54234, or phone: 414-854-4379; after July 10, phone: 414-854-4060.

The Heritage Ensemble: This delightful entourage of musicians both educate and entertain during July and August at Peninsula State Park's amphitheater. These family-oriented folk productions mix music with history in an outdoor setting, creating a combination that's hard to beat. Times are posted on the park bulletin boards, or call the park's visitor center for information.

The Peninsula Dance Program: Those wishing to hone their dancing skills will enjoy the Peninsula Dance Program offered by the University of Wisconsin Continuing Education in the Arts. Summer dance classes and performances are offered. For information and fees contact the UW Extension at: 608-263-8927.

Red Rooster Playhouse: A relatively new addition to Fish Creek's theater scene is the Red Rooster Playhouse, located south of the village on Highway 42. Local artist Steve Kastner and friends present marionette theater to children and adults alike in their all-weather theater each evening except Saturday from late June through Labor Day. For information and reservations phone: 414-868-2454.

Sunset Town Park: This small park is three blocks west of the Highway 42 stop sign where Main Street meets Green Bay. It offers a great view.

Clark Memorial Town Park: Another small park on the bay, this is a nice place to pretend you own one of the yachts visible from here.

Chambers Island Town Park: This island is about six miles offshore and is accessible by boat only. There's a pier on the east side where you can tie up, or you can drag your kayak up the sand beach. It's a day-use park only, but this 40-acre site makes a nice, isolated spot for a picnic.

Village of Ephraim *(pop. 309)*

If Fish Creek represents the heart of the northern Door Peninsula, Ephraim marks its soul. It is amid the white buildings and bluff-side churches on the sparkling bay that visitors develop a passion for this area and a longing to preserve it.

An unwritten law requiring that buildings in Ephraim be painted white or carry no paint at all has survived since the early Moravians settled on this harbor in the 1850s. You won't find a pub in this village either. As if not to tarnish the lily-white appearance of Ephraim, the village remains dry.

Taking its title from a popular biblical name meaning "the very fruitful" in Hebrew, Ephraim was first settled by Moravians seeking religious freedom in the Door Peninsula wilderness. Arriving in winter, these early settlers had no idea that under the snow and shallow soil lay a layer of limestone that would make farming a challenge. But clinging to the land and their deep-rooted faith they survived to carve out a niche on this beautiful bay shore.

Across the harbor, one can see 180-foot-high Eagle Bluff. For years a pair of eagles nested near this site and may have been responsible for the name given to this bay, Eagle Harbor. Horseshoe Island (formerly called Eagle Island) lies in the harbor. The natural U-shaped harbor on Horseshoe Island is said to have provided refuge to French explorer Jean Nicolet in 1630. Today it serves the same function for modern-day adventurers who drop anchor to admire the view or spend the night.

Scandinavian immigrants were also drawn to this village due to its resemblance to their homeland. Ephraim's Fyr (pronounced "fear") Ball Festival pays tribute to this heritage during a celebration marking the summer solstice. Bonfires are lit along the shore at dusk during a ceremony commemorating the arrival of summer with the burning of the winter witch. A local dignitary is crowned Fyr Ball Chieftan and a traditional fish boil rounds out the evening's entertainment.

Just south of the village lies the north entrance to Peninsula State Park and one of the most beautiful

PIONEER STORE

The Pioneer Store is an Ellison Bay landmark. It was built in 1900 by Charles Ruckert and served as the village post office when Mr. Ruckert was postmaster from 1903 to 1915. Its current owners have maintained its rustic atmosphere and timeless appeal.

104

golf courses in the Midwest. Teeing off from lime-stone bluffs, golfers will enjoy both the challenge and the beauty surrounding them on this 18-hole course. An errant five-iron may well land near the fairway totem pole that marks the 1931 burial site of Pota-watomi Chief Khaquados. Chief Khaquados was a di-rect descendant of Chief Onanquisse, a Potawatomi credited with saving the lives of starving French ex-plorers as they wintered on the peninsula in 1680. Chief Khaquados was said to have been so pleased with the totem pole, erected before his death, that he remarked, "This is the first time the white man not only kept his word, but has done more than he promised."

Ephraim's church stee-ples and white build-ings overlook Eagle harbor. An unwritten law in Ephraim man-dates that buildings in the village be painted white or carry no paint at all.

Ephraim shares an airport with the town of Gibraltar. It's located on Maple Grove Road south of Ephraim.

Library/Village Hall: Located on Highway 42 where it curves in downtown Ephraim. Phone: 414-854-2014.

Ephraim Information Center: For information write the center at Ephraim, WI 54211. Phone: 414-854-4426.

Anderson Museum: This is located on the north end of the village on Highway 42.

Anderson Dock Park: Located off Highway 42 at the north end of the village. There are boat slips here and a place for fishing, all with a great view of the Peninsula State Park bluffs.

Ephraim Playground: At the corner of Norway and Church streets you'll find tennis courts, a basketball court, playground equipment and picnic tables.

Ephraim Village Beach: The beach is off Highway 42 at the south end of the village. It's a sand beach with parking and has a nice view of the harbor.

A Walking Tour of Ephraim

Ephraim's rich history comes to life as you take a walking tour through the village. Beginning at the village hall in the center of town, a brief hike north along the bayshore will bring you to Anderson's Dock. Here, in 1859, Aaslag Anderson and a Mr. Peter Peterson purchased 150 acres from the Moravian church for $200. These two men built the dock and later the general store that served as the center of activity in this village. Today, the rustic building adjacent to the dock is painted with the various ship names that have docked here over the years, providing an interesting spectacle. The building houses the Francis Hardy Art Gallery, which is operated by a group of Ephraim residents as an art center. The Hardy Gallery is open to the public at designated hours. Across from the dock you'll find the old Anderson Homestead, which has recently been restored.

To continue your tour, walk up the hill to the east to Moravia Street. Turning right you'll be taking a picturesque walk through an arch of cedar and white birch leading to the Pioneer Schoolhouse. This village schoolhouse was built in 1869 and operated by the Ephraim Foundation as a museum open to the public. During summer this building houses the office of the Peninsula Music Festival. Nearby you'll find the Goodletson family homestead, dating back to the 1860s. Next to the Pioneer Schoolhouse is the Lutheran Church.

A winding walk north up County Q will bring you to Ephraim's present-day kindergarten and the village tennis and basketball courts. Continue south down Norway Street to Valentine Lane and you'll find the Moravian cemetery. A glimpse at the old monuments will open a chapter in Ephraim's past.

Heading down the hill again towards the bay will take you to the Ephraim Moravian Church, noted for its white steeple. The church, originally 40 feet by 24 feet by 16 feet in height, was moved from the shore to its present site. South of the Moravian parsonage is the site of Pastor Iverson's original home. Now in private ownership, the original limestone drywall in front of the home was built by Iverson himself.

A walk south along the shore takes you to the Ephraim public beach. You'll have a great view of the village and limestone cliffs of Peninsula State Park across the bay. Returning to the center of the village you'll pass a stone monument marking the first landing of Iverson and his Moravian followers. From here it's a short trip back to the village hall, which houses the public library. This impressive building reflects the Scandinavian heritage of Ephraim and provides an excellent vantage point to watch the sunset over Eagle Harbor.

Village of Sister Bay *(pop. 696)*

The village of Sister Bay lies in the shelter of the Sister Bluffs. These twin cliffs rise 130 and 190 feet

EPHRAIM ANCESTRY

Ephraim's history can be traced to the fjords of Norway. Early Moravians of Norwegian descent settled in Ephraim in 1853 and later built summer hotels to attract visitors.

above the bay shore, towering over a second pair of siblings in the bay called the Sister Islands.

This is the largest and busiest village north of Sturgeon Bay, and many of its current residents trace their roots to Scandinavians who settled this region in the 1860s. Among the Swedes who came was a massive woodcutter by the name of John A. "Long John" Johnson. Known for his insatiable appetite, legend has it that a local storekeeper bet the giant five dollars he couldn't eat five dozen eggs in one sitting. Long John took the bet on the condition the prize included a pint of whiskey. Long John is said to have eaten all the eggs, drunk the whiskey and gone home to top it off with a loaf of bread and a pail of milk.

As ax gave way to plow, woodcutters who chose to stay in Sister Bay took up either fishing or farming. On the Door Peninsula fishing was a year-round affair with fishermen making their way across the ice to cast their nets. The danger of this practice was illustrated in 1893, when nine men sailed their ice sleds about five miles across the unpredictable frozen bay. Wind sent the fishing party adrift on the bay when an ice floe broke from the mainland. Rescue by boat was hampered by high winds, and the nine were given up for dead. But three days later the wind shifted, and the ice floe was spotted on the horizon making its way toward shore. Near enough to jump for land, the fishermen were saved by the same cursed wind that had sent them sailing.

Today, Sister Bay is the center of population and commerce on the northern Door Peninsula. During summer its streets are filled with tourists shopping and gawking at the goats atop a local sod-roofed restaurant. Autumn finds people converging on Sister Bay during Fall Fest, held annually during the second weekend in October. This is the busiest festival on the Door Peninsula and reservations are highly recommended.

Despite the bustling streets and throngs of tourists, wildlife still manages to carve a niche just beyond the village limits. The 1988 harvest of a black bear by a Sister Bay bow hunter in northern Door County confirms this. Even though the bruin was taken legally, its death still ruffled the feathers of residents opposed to sanctioned hunting of the dozen or so bears still roaming wild in Door County.

Gateway Park: At the intersection of Highways 42 and 57, look for the log cabin housing the tourist information center. There is also a picnic area.

Sister Bay Advancement Association: For information write: P.O. Box 201, Sister Bay, WI 54234, or phone: 414-854-2812.

Sister Bay Village Park: Off Highway 42 in the center of town, this park offers a guarded sand and pebble beach and a dock.

Sand Bay Town Park: This five-acre park is located four miles northeast of Sister Bay. Take Highway 42 to Waters End Road, turn right (east) to north Sand Bay Lane. There's a beach on Lake Michigan.

Pebble Beach: Take Pebble Beach Road off Highway 42 at the southwestern edge of the village. As the name implies, this is a pebble, not sand, beach.

Village of Ellison Bay *(pop. 125)*

Ellison Bay unfolds like a beautiful painting as visitors arriving from the south crest 190-foot-high Ellison Bluff overlooking this quaint village. En route from Sister Bay, orchards fill the landscape with blossoms in late May, making this a perfect time to visit the tip of the peninsula.

Founded by John Ellison, a Dane who moved up the bay shore from Ephraim to make his fortune in 1863, the village has a long and rich history of catering to tourists. The annual Olde Ellison Bay Days celebration in late June continues this tradition with a rope pull, parade and fish boil. The simple recipe of fresh whitefish, potatoes and onions has been a Door Peninsula tradition since fishermen began casting their nets in these waters over a century ago.

Hiking either the Mink River Nature Conservancy or nearby Newport State Park is a great way to burn off the calories gained enjoying the whitefish feast.

Open to passive recreation, including hiking and cross-country skiing, both of these preserves demand delicate exploration.

The Clearing: A drive through town is not complete until motorists wind down scenic Garrett Bay Road, and if it's a Sunday afternoon, a visit to The Clearing should be high on your agenda. Long one of the best-kept secrets in Door County, The Clearing is the legacy of Chicago-based landscape architect Jens Jenson. This native Dane, at age 75, envisioned a "school of the soil" where aspiring landscape architects could gain hands-on experience at this 125-acre bluff's edge site located on the northern end of Ellison Bay. The Clearing celebrated its 50th anniversary in 1985 and offers classes in music, writing, nature studies, dance and literature. Far removed from the neighboring beaches, gift shops and campgrounds, students spend their evenings in limestone and wood dormitories, free of television, but filled with contemplation. The Clearing is open to visitors on Sunday afternoons, mid-May through October. Phone: 414-854-4088.

Ellison Bluff County Park: Three miles southwest of Ellison Bay on Highway 42, exit west on Porcupine Bay Road. Turn right on Ellison Bluff Road to the park. There's a spectacular view of Green Bay from the crest of Ellison Bluff. The 88-acre park also offers short hiking trails and picnic facilities.

Ellison Bay Municipal Dock and Ramp: This launch facility is off Highway 42 at the center of the village.

Ellison Bay Women's Club Park: Off Highway 42 at the south end of the village, this park offers a small beach, tennis courts and picnic facilities.

Europe Bay Town Park: Exit Highway 42 northeast of the village at Europe Bay Road and continue to the road's gravel conclusion. There's an excellent sand beach and picnic facilities, although parking is limited.

Newport State Park: Exit Highway 42 northeast of the village and follow the signs. There's a great beach here and a wilderness setting.

(opposite page)

Lady slippers lay their claim to the forest floor at The Clearing, an adult "school of the soil" in Ellison Bay.

LAKESHORE

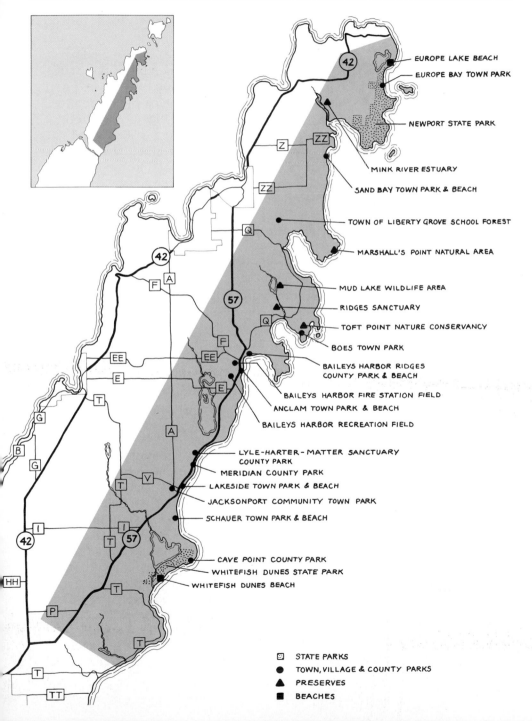

EUROPE LAKE BEACH
EUROPE BAY TOWN PARK
NEWPORT STATE PARK
MINK RIVER ESTUARY
SAND BAY TOWN PARK & BEACH
TOWN OF LIBERTY GROVE SCHOOL FOREST
MARSHALL'S POINT NATURAL AREA
MUD LAKE WILDLIFE AREA
RIDGES SANCTUARY
TOFT POINT NATURE CONSERVANCY
BOES TOWN PARK
BAILEYS HARBOR RIDGES COUNTY PARK & BEACH
BAILEYS HARBOR FIRE STATION FIELD
ANCLAM TOWN PARK & BEACH
BAILEYS HARBOR RECREATION FIELD
LYLE-HARTER-MATTER SANCTUARY COUNTY PARK
MERIDIAN COUNTY PARK
LAKESIDE TOWN PARK & BEACH
JACKSONPORT COMMUNITY TOWN PARK
SCHAUER TOWN PARK & BEACH
CAVE POINT COUNTY PARK
WHITEFISH DUNES STATE PARK
WHITEFISH DUNES BEACH

STATE PARKS
TOWN, VILLAGE & COUNTY PARKS
PRESERVES
BEACHES

Through the Windshield
AN OVERVIEW OF THE LAKESHORE

LAKE MICHIGAN

Lake Michigan is a freshwater lake with a maximum depth of 840 feet. Bottom types along Door County are predominantly bedrock, on exposed shores, and sand within the bayheads and shallow shores.

(overleaf)

The upper range light, erected in 1869, is one of a pair of beacons which provided a line of sight to guide ships past the treacherous sand bars of Baileys Harbor. This one served as home to the resident light keeper.

Sand dunes, wetlands, rocky ledges and isolated bays characterize Door County's untamed lakeshore. State parks, private preserves, islands and lighthouses provide the variety of scenery that keeps visitors returning year after year. Lacking the commercial development of the bayshore, lakeshore visitors tend to appreciate the cooler temperatures and wild shores that harbor rare orchids, waterfowl and coyote.

From Sturgeon Bay, lakeshore travelers will be following Highway 57 along Lake Michigan. You'll wish to bring a sweater along on this trek since the lake shore is frequently as much as ten degrees cooler than the bay side of the peninsula. If you're wishing to depart the well-traveled path, exit Highway 57 at County T, which leads to Glidden Drive. This is one of the most scenic drives in Door County and borders one of the last remaining privately held roadless areas on the peninsula. A number of dead-end roads with names like Deerpath and Arrowhead lanes provide public access to the lakeshore beach. In many cases, however, only the width of the road is public domain, so if you wish to take a walk down the beach, plan to get your feet wet to avoid trespassing on private property. Glidden Drive passes over Shivering Sands Creek, so named because the sand is said to quiver or "shiver" in the wind. This creek, fed by Maple Creek, drains Dunes Lake, one of the richest privately owned wetlands on the peninsula. Dunes Lake is a shallow drainage occupying an area submerged by ancient glacial Lake Nippissing. Nearly four hundred acres of wooded swampland border this lake, extending to the Lake Michigan shore.

Continuing north on Glidden Drive you'll pass over Whitefish Bay Creek. This picturesque creek drains Clark Lake. Bass, walleye, northern and perch constitute the fishery here, and if you're anxious to get your canoe wet, this 864-acre lake beckons. Just past Whitefish Bay Creek you'll reach the entrance to Whitefish Dunes State Park. If it's July or August, plan

114

on taking a swim. You'll find the best beach on the peninsula awaiting you. Fall and spring travelers will discover outstanding hiking trails complete with planked walkways to assist in climbing the 100-foot-high sand dunes. Winter visitors will find scenic cross-county ski trails and often the best snow conditions on the peninsula, thanks to the influence of Lake Michigan on winter storm patterns.

Travelers without the time or energy to follow Glidden Drive will find a clearly marked access road off Highway 57 leading to Whitefish Dunes State Park. Less than one mile from the Whitefish Dunes entrance, sandwiched between state park land, is Cave Point County Park. The thunderous waves of Lake Michigan have worn caves in the 30-foot-high cliff, and the landscape is inspiring regardless of the season. Since this is a county park, you won't need a state park sticker to park your car here to enjoy a picnic or begin a cross-country ski outing.

From the entrance of Whitefish Dunes State Park, scenic Cave Point Drive leads to Highway 57 just south of Jacksonport. Jacksonport is located on the 45th Meridian, halfway between the North Pole and the Equator. Some three hundred years ago, this area was a large Potawatomi Indian village known as Mechingan. When white settlers arrived here in the mid-1800s the great cedar forests that sheltered the Potawatomi fell to the ax and saw of logger Andrew Jackson, for whom the village is named. Today, Jacksonport is a pleasant lakeshore farming community with a fine sand beach that has attracted many vacation home owners. Most of the families who settled this region are of German ancestry, and they celebrate this heritage with the annual "Maifest." Lakeside Park is the center of Maifest activities, offering an excellent beach and plenty of room to polka.

Driving through the dense evergreen stand between Jacksonport and Baileys Harbor you'll pass over Hibbards Creek. Fishermen are attracted to its steelhead trout runs. Having driven 21 miles from Sturgeon Bay, you'll now be entering Baileys Harbor. Once a logging camp, shipping point and original Door County seat, Baileys Harbor is today a popular

WHITEFISH DUNES TROLLING

The near-shore areas of Lake Michigan adjacent to Whitefish Dunes State Park provide excellent fishing. Trolling and surf casting in April and May are popular methods of fishing for brown, brook and rainbow trout.

BJORKLUNDEN VID SJON

The Boynton estate, the complete name of which is "Bjork-lunden Vid Sjon," or "Birch Forest by the Water," in-cludes the Boyn-tons' residence, the family chapel, a workshop, a studio and a caretaker's home. The build-ings are situated on 325 acres of wooded land front-ing Lake Michigan.

resort community. The village is named after Captain Justice Bailey, who took refuge in its natural harbor in 1844. Today, fishing captains frequently launch their own excursions from this village, hoping to battle a chinook salmon, coho or trout.

Just south of the village at the end of Chapel Lane stands the famed Bjorklunden Chapel. This "sanctuary of peace" was hand-crafted in Norwegian-style architecture by Winifred and Donald Boynton. Today the chapel and grounds are maintained by Lawrence University and open Wednesday afternoons during the summer. At the north end of the village off Ridges Drive, a lovely sand beach invites a swim. This county park is adjacent to the world-renowned Ridges Sanctuary. The entrance to this private wildflower preserve can be found just north of Ridges Drive off Highway 57. The 900-acre natural garden is open to the public and protects some 17 wooded sand "ridges" and the wet swales that lie between them. These ancient ridges harbor over 25 species of orchids and such rare flowers such as the dwarf iris, arctic primrose and fringed gentian. Located on the Ridges Sanctuary are a pair of famous old rangelights providing a line of sight to guide ships into the harbor. These two synchronized beacons were built in 1870, replacing the original Baileys Harbor lighthouse that had served the port since 1852. The old rangelight residence once served as home to Ridges' naturalist Roy Lukes. In 1975 the old wooden light tower was completely restored by the Sanctuary, but today modern navigational aids have rendered the historic beacons obsolete.

Adjacent to Ridges Sanctuary, off Ridges Road, is Toft's Point Nature Conservancy. This magnificent 633-acre preserve encompasses virgin forest and untamed shoreline. In 1976, the University of Wisconsin, which administrates the property, attempted to have the gravel road winding through this site abandoned by the town to prevent motorized intrusion. To date this hasn't occurred and while a drive is still possible, hiking or skiing remains the best means of exploration.

Rolling out of Baileys Harbor you'll have the option

116

of cruising down County Q through a remote and intriguing portion of the peninsula. This pleasant road snakes through the Ridges Sanctuary, following Moonlight Bay before crossing Riebolts Creek. Before spilling into Lake Michigan, this stream drains Mud Lake, a 155-acre shallow pool surrounded by wetlands, cedar and aspen groves. Combined with adjacent Ridges Sanctuary and Toft Point, this eco-system has been designated a national landmark. Mud Lake is also a state wildlife area. Penetrating this rugged land can be difficult, adding to its unique appeal.

Continuing down Q you'll encounter the side road leading to Cana Island. A stone causeway, accessible by foot, makes Cana the most accessible of all Door County islands. An historic lighthouse awaits you. Time your visit between ten and five during the summer, so as not to disturb the resident caretakers. Winding back on Q, you'll be driving parallel to North Bay. North Bay is accessible by boat off North Bay Road via County ZZ at Sister Bay. This shallow, marshy bay provides a striking contrast to the limestone cliffs found on the peninsula's bayshore. Fishing for northern pike and bass is popular, but landing on the private shoreline is prohibited. County Q intersects with Highway 57 just south of Sister Bay. This busy village is the center of commerce in northern Door County, and its shops, restaurants and lodges provide a livelihood for the folks who call this part of the peninsula home.

STATE PARKS

Whitefish Dunes State Park

The entrance is well marked north of Sturgeon Bay off Highway 57. The address: Route 3, Sturgeon Bay, WI 54235; phone: 414-823-2400.

FACILITIES:
Whitefish Dunes is a day-use park, and no camping is allowed. There are pit toilets, picnic areas and an excellent sand beach. A state park vehicle admission sticker is required if you park. These are available annually or daily, and nonresidents pay more than Wisconsin residents.

RECREATION:
The park is open year-round and offers an observation deck, hiking, swimming, picnicking and cross-country skiing.

The swimming beach at Whitefish Dunes State Park is paradise with a lakeside view. Each summer hordes of sun worshippers flock to this beach to work on their tans. The parking lot can accommodate only a limited number of vehicles, so if you plan a mid-July visit, hit the beach before the prime rays do.

If you left your sun block at home, a hike on the park trails may be just the ticket to recharge your batteries. You'll leave the crowds behind and be treated to a saunter among the largest sand dunes in Wisconsin.

The ancient sand dunes found here trace their beginning to the glaciers when a minor "dent" in the Door Peninsula shoreline became the basin of Clark Lake and Whitefish Bay. Over time lake action built up a barrier separating Clark Lake from the bay. Wind action then took over, building the dunes higher and moving them gradually further inland. Plant life eventually stabilized some of the dunes, while others are still considered unstabilized. The stabilized dunes provide a delicate home for plant colonies attempting to eke out an existence in this harsh environment. The largest of the dunes, "Old Baldy," rises over 90 feet above lake level.

DUNES VEGETATION
Whitefish Dunes hosts a variety of plant communities because of its unique environment. A boreal forest climate is found along the lakeshore while near-desert conditions exist behind the dunes.

Hikers will find an excellent trail system by which to observe the dunes. Rope and wood planks traverse many of the trails in the park, easing the strain of climbing the steep sand dunes and protecting the delicate and endangered species that cling to them. Hikers are asked to remain on the trails, respecting this fragile environment.

WHITEFISH DUNES STATE PARK

HIKING TRAILS

The **red trail** (2.8 miles) is a five-star trail that offers hikers an excellent example of everything Whitefish

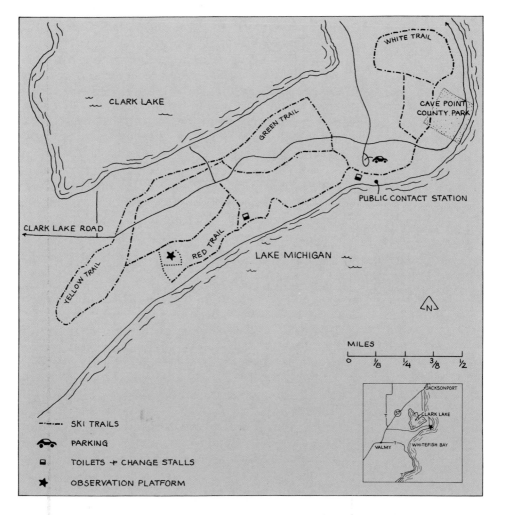

CLARK LAKE

WHITE TRAIL

CAVE POINT COUNTY PARK

GREEN TRAIL

PUBLIC CONTACT STATION

CLARK LAKE ROAD

RED TRAIL

LAKE MICHIGAN

YELLOW TRAIL

N

MILES

0   ⅛   ¼   ⅜   ½

JACKSONPORT

CLARK LAKE

VALMY   WHITEFISH BAY

- - - ·-·   SKI TRAILS

🚗   PARKING

▪   TOILETS + CHANGE STALLS

★   OBSERVATION PLATFORM

Dunes State Park has to offer. Beginning at the parking area you'll first wind through a forest in the shadow of the magnificent sand dunes that separate the red trail from Lake Michigan. The trail then provides access to Lake Michigan beach, but those who continue will reach Old Baldy, at 93 feet the tallest dune in the park. An observation deck on Old Baldy provides an unbeatable view of Lake Michigan and, on a clear day, Clark Lake as well.

The **green trail** (1.8 miles) follows the forested base of an old dune where hikers can wonder how a forest could sprout from this sandy soil. Winding back through a lowland area, walkers will wander through hemlock and white pine before returning through a beech-maple forest.

At just over four miles, the **yellow trail** is the longest trail in the park, and hikers have a chance to enjoy the green trail before the yellow trail branches off for those wishing to continue. The terrain on the yellow trail changes to an almost desert-like area before returning through a cool red pine plantation and wooded dunes.

First-time visitors will not want to miss the **white trail** since it leads to Cave Point County Park. Here, visitors can often witness Lake Michigan pounding the limestone cliffs in a thunderous roar.

CROSS-COUNTRY SKI TRAILS

Cross-country skiers also use the 11 miles of hiking trails that wind through the park. Winter storms often deposit generous snowfall on Whitefish Dunes State Park thanks to the influence of Lake Michigan on this shoreline preserve. Skiers searching for early-season snow may encounter bare fields until arriving at this park where trails with adequate snow cover can sometimes be found. You can check first by calling 414-823-2400.

All of the ski trails begin at the greeting center and most cater to beginners. Sections of the yellow, red and green trails merit a more difficult rating as skiers return to the parking lot, but there is nothing too challenging to contend with.

120

Newport State Park

The entrance is five miles east of Ellison Bay off Highway 42 and is well marked. The address: 475 S. Newport Lane, Ellison Bay, WI 54210; phone: 414-854-2500.

FACILITIES:
This year-round park offers 16 backpacking campsites. There is no vehicle access to campsites. There are pit toilets and a central water supply. Reservations are recommended in July and August on official forms, and only the even-numbered sites are reservable. A state park vehicle admission sticker is required to park at Newport. Both annual and day stickers are available and nonresidents pay more than Wisconsin residents. 2,200 acres.

RECREATION:
Places and facilities for hiking, swimming, sea kayaking, canoeing, cross-country skiing and picnicking are provided.

Wild, rugged, peaceful and inspiring, Newport State Park beckons. Visitors planning to spend the night will have to hoist a pack or pull a paddle to reach their campsite. No motor vehicles are allowed off the paved road and camping is restricted to hike-in sites. The wilderness atmosphere makes Newport unique.

Hikers will delight in the 28 miles of marked trails that wind through the woods and snake along seven miles of spectacular Lake Michigan shoreline. Sea kayakers will find sandy beaches on which to launch and land, and canoeists have campsite access to one of the most beautiful inland lakes on the Door Peninsula.

Day visitors will relish the 3,000-foot-long sand beach, and families will enjoy picnicking along the scenic shore. Crowds are rarely a problem at Newport, and swimmers willing to hike the shoreline are certain to find plenty of room to spread out their beach blankets.

Camping at Newport State Park is a four-season affair. As summer gives way to autumn, hunters search for white-tail deer during Wisconsin's gun deer season. Winter brings its own special magic to campers

SCIENTIFIC AREA

Approximately 140 acres within Newport State Park have been designated as the "Newport Conifer-Hardwoods Scientific Area." Located in the southern end of the park, the area was established to preserve and protect a good example of mixed conifers and northern hardwoods.

122

willing to stretch out on a blanket of snow. Spring makes a slow arrival on the peninsula; visitors enjoy the sense of renewal even though the trails may be soggy.

Campers must stay at designated campsites where they'll find fire rings, pit toilets and marked tent pads. The 16 campsites are all accessible by foot with the closest about one mile from the parking area. The two campsites on Europe Lake are accessible by canoe as well as by foot, but you can't park overnight at the Europe Lake boat launch. Someone will have to hike out and move the car to the state park parking

SNOWMOBILES PROHIBITED
Snowmobiles are outlawed from Newport State Park, but there are excellent cross-country ski trails and opportunities for snowshoeing.

NEWPORT STATE PARK

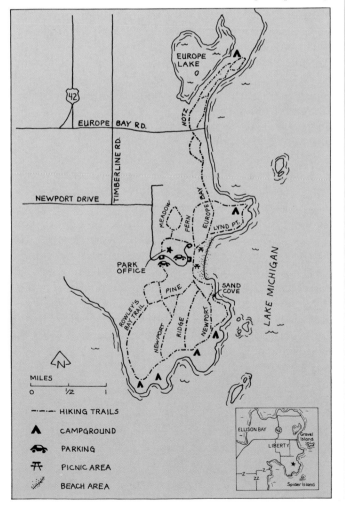

123

area. Paddlers willing to brave the unpredictable weather and waves of Lake Michigan have access to all of Newport's shoreline campsites by canoe or kayak. Canoeists should use extreme caution, leaving the beach only under favorable skies and a promising forecast, and should have an alternate plan for getting out if conditions turn nasty.

History buffs will enjoy searching for signs of Newport's early settlement. In the 1880s Newport was a thriving town. Settled in the 1870s by logger Hans Johnson, the community bustled with a general store, post office, dock and sawmill. When the majestic white pine trees fell to the ax, the logging jobs disappeared with them. Plans to develop streets were scrapped, and in 1919, as Newport floundered, the land was sold to Chicago investor Ferdinand Hotz.

"Without the slightest doubt the most outstanding state park possibility along the Lake Michigan shore." So reads the reference to Door County's Newport area in a 1946 study by the Wisconsin Planning Board and the Wisconsin Conservation Department. But even following such a glowing description, it was not until September 24, 1964, that a state park became a reality. The park was named "Europe Bay State Park" because original studies had recommended inclusion of acreage on Lake Michigan's Europe Bay and inland Europe Lake. When these plans went temporarily awry, a name change to Newport State Park was deemed appropriate. When the state of Wisconsin purchased the Hotz property, it gradually removed what few buildings remained. Today, observant visitors can find the outlines of the post office in the beach area as lilac bushes and grapevines claim the hopes and dreams of a bygone era.

Thankfully, plans to include acreage on both Europe Bay and Europe Lake were not easily forgotten. In 1978, the state acquired a magnificent wooded isthmus separating Europe Lake from Lake Michigan. Known as the Hotz tract, the 170-acre parcel included a cabin that has since been removed, leaving only memories of a pioneer's past.

With 28 miles of marked hiking trails and 16 backpack campsites, Newport State Park is the most pop-

ular destination for backpackers on the peninsula. The terrain is wild and rugged to behold, but gentle and mellow to hike.

HIKING TRAILS

Newport Trail: This trail is the longest (4.5 miles), widest and most used trail in the park. Easily hiked in three hours, the trail forms a loop along old logging roads still used for park maintenance. Beginning from either beach parking lot, hikers will wind through low-lying areas thick with white cedar, balsam fir and hemlock. Keep a lookout for the huge virgin white pines near the intersection with the Sand Cove Trail, and you'll have an idea of how this area looked during the last century.

Europe Bay Trail: Beginning at parking lot 3, the Europe Bay Trail (3.25 miles) heads north along an old logging trail through maple and beech forests to Europe Bay. Past the Fern Trail junction, ancient sand ridges run parallel to the beach. Between the ridges water has been trapped, forming tiny, delicate bog communities. These ridges are former shores of a receding glacial lake. Just to the east of the trail is Europe Bay with a 1.5-mile-long sand beach that provides a panorama that includes Lake Michigan, Death's Door Passage and Plum and Detroit islands.

Hotz Trail: The varied terrain makes this two-mile trail a park favorite. The trail begins on the north side of Europe Bay Road (accessible off Europe Bay Trail) and passes through a forest of red pine, oak and beech trees. As you climb the sand ridge you will see Europe Lake on your left. It is believed this lake was a bay of Lake Michigan until wave action deposited sand that today forms the ridge separating the two bodies of water. Over a mile of the eastern shore of this 274-acre lake is part of Newport State Park. As you continue down the trail you'll find several points where both Europe Lake and Lake Michigan are visible. Your return trip takes you to the Lake Michigan shore, adding to the beauty and variety of this glorious hike.

TEMPERATURE
The average high temperature for Newport in July is a balmy 80 degrees but the low drops down to 57. During January, high temp is 27 degrees, the low a chilly 10.

Lynd Point Trail: This two-mile trail provides access to campsites 1 and 2 off the Europe Bay Trail while taking hikers along the rocky Lake Michigan shoreline. The tiny island to the northeast of Lynd Point is Gravel Island National Wildlife Refuge, home to nesting gulls, cormorants and shorebirds.

Fern Trail: The short (.75 miles) Fern Trail begins at lot 3 near the picnic area and winds through an old spruce plantation. Be on the lookout for wildflowers in the spring and summer.

Meadow Trail: This trail (two miles) is Newport's self-guided nature trail. Beginning at the visitor contact station near the park entrance, the loop includes 36 trail stations to help you identify trees, flowers and wildlife.

The Pine Trail loop (two miles) provides park visitors the best opportunity to spot white-tail deer grazing in the open areas at dusk. Reached from the visitor's station near the park entrance, this loop circles through a 50-year-old spruce plantation, hidden meadows and forest.

Rowleys Bay Trail: The 2.5-mile Rowleys Bay Trail connects the Pine Trail with campsites at Varney's Point. The trail leads through meadows and fields that are slowly being reclaimed by the forest after being cleared for crops.

Sand Cove Trail: This is a short (one mile) track that cuts off of the Newport Trail and follows the lakeshore to Sand Cove, a beautiful, secluded sand beach that beckons overheated hikers to take a swim.

CROSS-COUNTRY SKI TRAILS

These hiking trails are recombined to become longer Nordic trails in the winter. Generally they are flat, easy and forgiving even for beginners, but northern portions of the white trail near Europe Lake lead to an exhilarating, albeit brief, hill to be avoided by rookies. Snow cover is best from December to mid-March, but if in doubt, call first: 414-854-2500. Even if snowfall is poor, pac boots will provide for a pleasant hike in this year-round wonderland.

SUNSHINE
The odds of encountering sunshine favor campers at Newport from May through September. In November and December sunshine averages only 40%, and the remaining months, somewhere in between.

(opposite page)

Serenity can be found at Newport State Park.

PARK WINDS

April and November are the windiest months at Newport State Park. Prevailing winds are typically from the northwest or the southwest, with the exception of early spring when northeast winds are predominate.

The **white trail** (seven miles) begins at parking lot 3. Start on the yellow trail before joining the white loop as you head toward Europe Lake. This trail follows the path of an old logging road through maple and beech forest. It is the longest single trail in the park, and offers great views of both frozen Europe Lake and icy cold Lake Michigan. An alternative starting point is reached off Europe Bay Road with access to the ski trail just west of Europe Bay Town Park.

Also from parking lot 3, the **red loop** (five miles) winds through a forest of white cedar, balsam fir, hemlock and white pine. The trail follows an old logging road that becomes the main thoroughfare for hikers during the summer months. The going is easy and the trail is pleasant, forming an easy connection to the blue loop for an extended journey.

You can pick up the **blue loop** (five miles) from parking lot 1. This picturesque loop takes skiers along the shores of Lake Michigan through a cedar forest before reaching Varney's Point. The wind often whips along this stretch of shoreline and the trail can become icy during periods of freeze and thaw.

The short **orange trail** (two miles), accessible from lot 1 only, takes skiers along the park's self-guided nature trail. The loop winds through cedar swamp and hardwood forest before returning to the parking lot.

The **yellow trail** (one mile) is a nice loop for beginners. As the trail circles through an old spruce plantation, novices will get a feel for the natural beauty of the park and the serenity of Nordic skiing.

(opposite page)

Rocky cliffs meet Lake Michigan on Door County's rugged lakeshore.

TOWN, VILLAGE AND COUNTY PARKS

Cave Point County Park *(18.6 acres)*

Cave Point County Park is well known for its wave-worn limestone ledges, underwater caves and stirring view of Lake Michigan. When the waves of Lake Michigan are crashing against the caves, water erupts from the limestone cliffs in a thunderous roar, creating a magnificent scene. Fishermen, skilled scuba divers, experienced sea kayakers, photography buffs, and nature observers find the park a great delight. Facilities include picnic tables, fire rings and parking for about 20 cars. Whitefish Dunes State Park borders this preserve on three sides.

Schauer Town Park *(1.5 acres)*

Schauer Town Park is located just north of Whitefish Dunes State Park and provides public boat access to Lake Michigan with a one-lane boat ramp. There is parking for about eight cars with trailers.

Lakeside Town Park *(3.3 acres)*

Located off Highway 57, in the heart of Jacksonport, Lakeside Town Park provides a pleasant sand swimming beach and a large grassy lawn on which to relax. This park is the center of activity during the annual Maifest celebration held each May. Playground equipment, grills and parking facilities are available. Attempts to maintain the boat launch ramp have been generally unsatisfactory because shifting sand continues to cover the ramp.

POTAWATOMI VILLAGE

The Potawatomi Indians had a large village known as "Mechingin" in the vicinity of the present-day village of Jacksonport.

Jacksonport Community Town Park
(10 acres)

Located west of the village center, the Jacksonport Community Town Park provides a lighted softball field and a pair of tennis courts. The grounds house

the town hall and the fire station as well. This is a pleasant site to take in a baseball game when players from the Door County summer baseball league step up to bat.

Meridian County Park *(92 acres)*

Meridian County Park is the second-largest county park in the Door County park system. A wayside on Highway 57 provides access to this undeveloped preserve, but its rugged nature makes exploration difficult. The wayside is maintained by the State Department of Transportation and includes restrooms and picnic facilities. This heavily wooded park is wet and marshy, providing excellent wildlife habitat. An old logging road through the property has been converted to a snowmobile trail. This park is adjacent to the Lyle-Harter-Matter Sanctuary.

Lyle Harter-Matter Sanctuary County Park *(40 acres)*

Donated to Door County in 1945 as a sanctuary, this 40-acre tract contiguous to Meridian County Park is completely undeveloped. This preserve is not served by a road. A magnificent high sand dune runs through the preserve, and a beautiful forest canopy of both deciduous and coniferous species covers most of the property. A marsh is also found on the preserve, creating an excellent undisturbed habitat for wildlife.

Baileys Harbor Recreation Field *(27 acres)*

The Baileys Harbor Recreation Field is noted for its fine baseball diamond, complete with fencing, bleachers, batter's cage and concession stand.

Anclam Town Park *(1 acre)*

Centrally located in Baileys Harbor, adjacent to Highway 57, Anclam Park provides a sand swimming beach

and a one-lane boat ramp providing access to Lake Michigan. A protective breakwater juts into the lake. Playground equipment, picnic tables and a grill are provided for those wishing to enjoy a picnic.

Baileys Harbor Fire Station Field

(1.6 acres)

Located adjacent to the fire station in Baileys Harbor, this park offers a pair of blacktop tennis courts, a grass field and parking for about one dozen cars.

Baileys Harbor Ridges County Park

(30 acres)

This park is famous for its two rangelight houses, used to provide a line of sight for mariners entering Baileys Harbor in bygone days. The houses still stand, but the original lights have been removed and modern directional rangelights have been installed elsewhere on the property by the Coast Guard. The rangelights are considered historical landmarks.

A fine sand beach is located on the harbor side of Ridges Drive and is popular for both swimming and sunning. A parking lot has ample room for those using the beach or hiking along trails that lead to the adjacent Ridges Sanctuary.

In 1972, Door County officials leased the property north of Ridges Drive to the Ridges Sanctuary for 20 years. This group now maintains the property and the rangelight houses.

(opposite page)

A woodland garden blankets the forest floor.

Boes Town Park *(.15 acres)*

This small park provides boat access to Moonlight Bay, offering a launch ramp with a removable pier. The site is small but pleasantly wooded. Parking is available for only two cars, so if you're planning an outing on Moonlight Bay, plan on arriving early.

Town of Liberty Grove School Forest

(60 acres)

The 60-acre Town of Liberty Grove Plantation Forest is located southwest of Sister Bay off Old Stage Road. This unmarked woodlot is publicly owned but difficult to explore because its boundaries are not defined. It is, however, a welcome tract of green space and it is comforting to know it will remain a visual oasis for travelers and a permanent refuge for plants and wildlife.

OLD RUGGED CROSS SITE

Father Louis Andre raised a wooden cross on Rowleys Bay near the mouth of the Mink River. This was a site of worship for Indian converts.

Sand Bay Town Park *(4 acres)*

An excellent sand beach and a beautiful view of Spider Island and Newport State Park characterize Sand Bay Town Park. Located at the intersection of Sand Bay Road and Water's End Road, this secluded beach has a wooded shore and parking for about six or seven cars. Picnic tables and grills are provided. This park provides an excellent free public launch to kayakers wishing to explore the Mink River Estuary. After launching, paddle north, past Rowleys Bay, about one half mile to the mouth of this Nature Conservancy preserve.

Europe Bay Town Park *(2 acres)*

This secluded sand beach is surrounded by Newport State Park and provides convenient access to one of the finest stretches of white sand on the peninsula. A gravel road leads to the beach. Watch for the small sign as you make the final turn into Newport State Park. The pleasantly wooded grounds here are perfect for a picnic, and the beach provides an excellent launch site for kayakers.

PRESERVES

Mink River Estuary

The preserve is on Rowleys Bay, southeast of Ellison Bay. Exit Highway 42 north of Ellison Bay at Newport Drive and watch for the Nature Conservancy marker as the road takes a sharp left. Also accessible from Ellison Bay by taking Mink River Road, which takes you to the southern part of the preserve. From Sister Bay take Highway 42 north to County Z and turn right. Follow County Z to Mink River Road.

FACILITIES:
A day-use area, the preserve is open year-round for observation by foot or canoe.

RECREATION:
Canoeing, sea kayaking, bird-watching, fishing and hiking.

The Mink River is one of the Door Peninsula's geographic wonders. Paddlers viewing this ancient wetland for the first time are taken by its pristine beauty and true wilderness character.

The Nature Conservancy recognizes this natural sanctuary as one of the few high-quality estuaries remaining in the United States. An estuary is an area at the mouth of a river where the current meets the tide. Here the Mink River meets Lake Michigan at Rowleys Bay, creating a rich aquatic freshwater estuary.

Alkaline springs feed the Mink River as it flows to Rowleys Bay. The Mink River is an important spawning area for fish. The estuary is also a critical migration site for birds, including the Cooper's hawk, a threatened species in Wisconsin. In fact, the Nature Conservancy estimates that over 200 bird species may pass through the area annually. Other wildlife including beaver, muskrat and white-tail deer make their home in this unique wetland.

Various unconnected parcels of land, owned and managed by the Nature Conservancy of Wisconsin, make up the preserve. Hikers entering the sanctuary will find springs and streams that saturate the forest

ROWLEYS BAY
Rowleys Bay is noted for its excellent smallmouth bass fishing. It also provides boaters access to the Mink River.

floor as they trickle toward the river. The upland forest gradually gives way to lowland cedar, and as you near the river, marshland prevails. Two plant species threatened with extinction in Wisconsin grow wild here: the dune thistle and the dwarf lake iris. Bulrush, a marsh plant found in abundance here, serves to protect the inland plant communities by withstand-

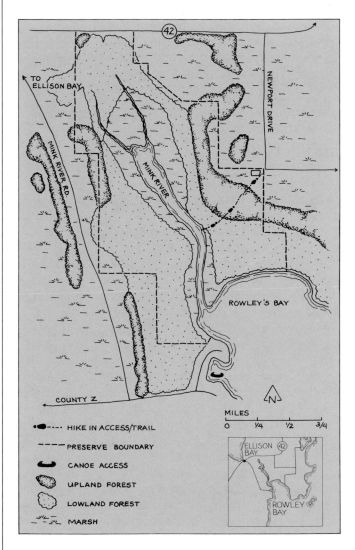

136

ing the constant wave and current action caused by Lake Michigan.

Today, visitors to the Mink River Estuary will find this ecosystem is much the same as when Potawatomi Indians inhabited this region more than a century ago. The Nature Conservancy is working to insure that it stays that way. To date 769 acres actually make up the preserve with a protection goal of 1,500 acres.

Ridges Sanctuary

Take Highway 57 north of Baileys Harbor to County Q.

FACILITIES:
The Ridges Sanctuary is a year-round facility offering hiking trails, a nature center and an observation platform.

RECREATION:
Guided nature hikes, bird-watching and hiking.

The Ridges Sanctuary is an outstanding natural classroom. This private nature preserve was established in 1937 by visionary conservationists "concerned for the future of the botanically rich area lying between Baileys Harbor and Moonlight Bay," according to the sanctuary trail guide. Time seems to be measured not in minutes and hours at the Ridges Sanctuary, but rather in eons and epochs. The trails follow some of the 17 ancient sand dune ridges formed as Lake Michigan advanced and retreated through the ages.

In 1936 plans were underway to build a trailer park here. With the advent of modern navigational techniques, the federal government had no more use for the 40-acre rangelight preserve that provided a line of sight to guide ships into Baileys Harbor. The land was deeded to the county for the park.

Local conservationists Jens Jenson and Emma Toft led the fight to preserve the ridges. Local legend has it that "Miss Emma" threw herself in front of a bulldozer to stop the trailer park, but in fact the battle was won through persuasion and reason as Toft convinced the county to turn the land over to the Ridges Sanctuary group. The original 40 acres has grown into a 910-acre

RIDGES RANGELIGHTS
A lighthouse was built on Baileys Harbor in 1852, but in 1870 it was replaced by two separate, synchronized beacons known as rangelights. These lights once consisted of kerosene lanterns magnified by thick lenses. They have been restored, but are no longer in service.

wildflower preserve with some 2,800 members supporting it. Today the public is welcome even though the sanctuary receives no tax dollars and purchases its own land for preservation. The sanctuary has the additional status of being recognized today as a national natural landmark by the Department of the Interior.

Most travelers time their visits to coincide with one of the May-to-October tours guided by sanctuary naturalists. Many are drawn by the 28 species of native orchids found growing in this botanical wonderland. Early June is the best time to see the Ridges Sanctuary's dwarf iris, gay wings and arctic primrose in bloom. Late June finds the orchids in bloom.

In addition to the wide variety of wildflowers growing here, over a dozen plant species on Wisconsin's endangered and threatened list call the sanctuary home. A self-guided tour is available for the independent visitor, but those venturing on the trails are asked not to pick the flowers or disturb the wildlife.

Toft Point Nature Conservancy

From Baileys Harbor turn right on Ridge Road at the north end of the village. Just over the small creek, turn left on the small, unmarked one-lane road. There is room for only a few cars at the gate. In winter, park on Ridge Road (if possible) and ski down the small town road to the lakeshore.

FACILITIES:
Hiking and cross-country ski trails are open year-round.

RECREATION:
The conservancy is open to the public for passive recreation including bird-watching, nature hikes and skiing.

An unspoiled tract of virgin timber and untamed shoreline awaits visitors to Toft Point on Moonlight Bay. Thanks to the Nature Conservancy and the remarkable Emma Toft, the deep, dark and intriguing forest that "Miss Emma" cherished shall remain wild forever.

(opposite page)

Tamaracks and reed grass border low lying swales at the Ridges Sanctuary, a world famous wildflower preserve.

Adjacent to Ridges Sanctuary, the original 275-acre Toft Point Natural Area was acquired by the Nature Conservancy in two separate tracts beginning in 1976. The acquisition was contingent on the stipulation that Miss Toft be allowed to remain in her "Mud Bay" home, as she called it, as long as she was willing and able. Those who knew Miss Emma tell tales of her scolding hikers audacious enough to pick flowers growing wild on the adjacent Ridges Sanctuary. "Sir," she was heard to say, "if you pick all these flowers there'll be none for others to enjoy." In 1982, the feisty guardian of Moonlight Bay died at age 91, bequeathing to all the natural treasure she had fought to preserve.

Expansion of the Toft Point Natural Area was accomplished in 1976. A 325-acre contiguous tract was purchased by the Nature Conservancy from the Ajax Lumber Company and the Lighthouse Point Development Corporation. The preserve now encompasses 633 acres, including 2.5 miles of wild Lake Michigan shoreline on Moonlight Bay. The preserve has been turned over to the University of Wisconsin–Green Bay and today serves as a research site and a natural classroom, as well as being open to the public for passive recreation.

MOONLIGHT BAY

Moonlight Bay is popular among perch, bass and pike fishermen. An inlet here provides canoe access to Mud Lake.

Mud Lake Wildlife Area

From Baileys Harbor, take Highway 57 north to County Q. Turn right (east) and take County Q 2.5 miles to Reibolt's Creek, then canoe one mile upstream to Mud Lake. Or, just across Reibolt's Creek, follow Sunrise Road north 1.2 miles, then park and hike down the road to the unimproved landing on Mud Lake.

FACILITIES:
The wildlife area is open year-round with canoe access.

RECREATION:
Hiking, canoeing, bird-watching, hunting (in season) and cross-country skiing.

140

RIDGES
SANCTUARY
TOFT POINT
MUD LAKE

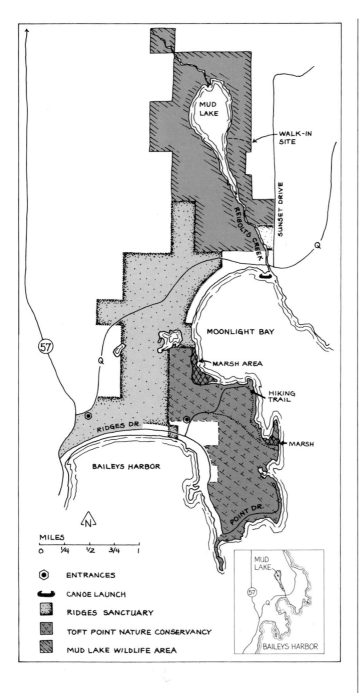

MUD
LAKE

WALK-IN
SITE

REIBOLTS CREEK

SUNSET DRIVE

Q

MOONLIGHT BAY

MARSH AREA

HIKING
TRAIL

57

Q

RIDGES DR.

MARSH

BAILEYS HARBOR

POINT DR.

N

MILES

0   ¼   ½   ¾   1

ENTRANCES

CANOE LAUNCH

RIDGES SANCTUARY

TOFT POINT NATURE CONSERVANCY

MUD LAKE WILDLIFE AREA

MUD
LAKE

57

Q

BAILEYS HARBOR

Mud Lake Wildlife Area is an outstanding resource characterized by its remote setting and peaceful, undisturbed atmosphere.

The lake itself is a shallow 155-acre drainage surrounded by extensive second-growth white cedar swamp. Canoeing provides the best access to the area, but many visitors hike in as well. Drained by Reibolt's Creek, Mud Lake provides one of the few remaining natural waterfowl production areas on the Door Peninsula.

The large size and remote character of this natural area provide habitat for species requiring large tracts of undisturbed wilderness including black bear, coyote and bobcat. Visitors may also encounter whitetail deer standing chest-high in Reibolt's Creek, or ruffed grouse exploding from thick cover. Birdwatchers may find wood ducks, pileated woodpeckers or even an occasional sharp-shinned hawk, known to nest in the adjacent Ridges Sanctuary.

Mud Lake has a maximum depth of five feet, though most of the lake is less than three feet deep. It is about 1.35 miles long and about a half mile wide. The largest of the three unnamed streams that enter Mud Lake has its outlet in the northwest corner of the lake and is about 2.5 miles long.

The state of Wisconsin began acquiring property for the Mud Lake Wildlife Area in 1966. The major landholder was Leeland Thorp, who owned 1,040 acres surrounding the lake and wished it preserved as a wildlife habitat. Since then, over 1,000 acres of the preserve have been designated a state scientific area. Further, Mud Lake Wildlife Area, Ridges Sanctuary and Toft Point in combination have been designated a national natural landmark by the Department of the Interior.

Marshall's Point Natural Area

Marshall's Point State Natural Area is located in a remote setting on North Bay and is surrounded by an exclusive private development. Access to the area is limited by an iron gate opened by electronic code.

Permission to explore this preserve is required from the Wisconsin Department of Natural Resources, and currently, barring the permission of its surrounding property owners, a boat will be required to visit. Contact the superintendent at Peninsula State Park for details (phone: 414-868-3258).

Marshall's Point is a beautiful, remote peninsula that juts into North Bay. Once targeted as a Wisconsin State Park due to its unique character and wilderness setting, Marshall's Point today is privately owned with the exception of a 110-acre parcel along the Lake Michigan shore. The parcel, dedicated as a State Natural Area, is held in public stewardship to protect the "unique boreal forest type that exists along the Lake Michigan shoreline, reflecting the influences of the near to surface limestone bedrock." It is considered the best remaining undisturbed site of its kind in Wisconsin.

Access to this Natural Area is extremely limited. Permission from the Department of Natural Resources is required to visit the site, and even with permission access is difficult because the parcel is surrounded by private land protected by a locked gate. Because the rocky shore can be hazardous to motorboats, a sea kayak may be the best mode of visitation. Serious students of the environment will find their access efforts rewarded when they discover the various threatened and endangered plant species, including *Iris lacustris,* clinging to life in this harsh lakeshore setting. The deep forest includes maple, beech and cedar trees that give way to a rocky shore harboring pioneering plants attempting to gain a foothold in the calcareous rock. The private land surrounding the preserve was once developed as an 18-hole golf course, but now nature is reclaiming the fairways and whitetail deer roam where golfers once played.

NORTH BAY

North Bay is an important spawning area for whitefish and 11 other fish species. Anglers enjoy fishing for smallmouth bass, northern pike and yellow perch in this relatively protected bay.

BEACHES

Whitefish Bay Dunes Beach

The glorious dunes at Whitefish Bay have long been a favorite haunt among local beachcombers. The water temperature is cooler than on the bay side of the peninsula, but the sizzling sand on a hot summer day can quickly comfort shivering swimmers. When the whitecaps are breaking, there is no better beach on Door Peninsula for body surfing, but use caution. Rip currents claimed the life of a swimmer here shortly before the park staff outlawed swimming at the far end of the beach.

Take Highway 57 north of Sturgeon Bay. Turn right at Whitefish Bay Road to Whitefish Dunes State Park. A vehicle admission sticker is required.

Schauer Park Beach

Bicyclists enjoying the scenic roads surrounding Whitefish Dunes State Park will find swimming opportunities adjacent to the boat ramp off Schauer Town Park. This tiny beach is no substitute for the wonderful sand of Whitefish Dunes, but when you're hot and tired it's a pleasant discovery.

Jacksonport Lakeside Beach

It's not surprising that Potawatomi Indians had a large village near Jacksonport when you consider they had a comfortable sand beach on which to camp. This beach and the surrounding park is a busy place during the annual Jacksonport Maifest celebration, but typically it's a quiet, comforting place to sun and swim.

Anclam Town Beach

Easy access to the center and a great view of Baileys Harbor make the Anclam Town Beach a convenient place for a quick swim. Located off Highway 57, the beach is protected by a large breakwater that juts into Lake Michigan.

DUNE BUILDING

Vast amounts of sand erodes from the shoreline and dunes during Lake Michigan's high-water periods. As the waters recede, the expanse of beach increases and the fine sand particles are exposed to the wind, beginning anew the process of dune-building.

(opposite page)

Chasing those lake-shore waves at Ridges County Park in Baileys Harbor.

144

Baileys Harbor Ridges Beach

This local beach is a favorite of those wishing to beat the crowds on a hot August day. Located off County Q, a portion of this park is leased to the Ridges Sanctuary.

Sand Bay Park Beach

Not to be confused with the private resort of the same name in southern Door County, Sand Bay Beach is located just south of Rowleys Bay in the northeastern corner of the county. This secluded beach is located at the intersection of Sand Bay Road and Water's End Road. It offers delightful swimming and a great view of Newport State Park and Spider Island. This is also a convenient place to launch a sea kayak for exploration of the nearby Mink River.

Europe Bay Town Park Beach

Easy access, shallow water and a beautiful natural setting characterize the beach at Europe Bay Town Park. The town of Liberty Grove has managed to maintain the rustic beauty of this beach by keeping development to a minimum and resisting the temptation to pave the gravel road to this local gem. Sun worshippers looking for elbow room need only head down the beach to adjacent Newport State Park. Here you'll find peace, quiet, sand and sun with a lush green forest at your back and a sweet-water sea nipping your toes. Parking is limited here, so plan to arrive early if you hope to stake a claim.

Exit Highway 42 north of Ellison Bay at the turn-off to Newport State Park on Europe Bay Road. Follow Europe Bay Road until it turns to gravel, concluding at the beach parking area.

Europe Lake Beach

Swimmers who can't quite muster the courage to brave the chilly waters of Lake Michigan will find Europe Lake a pleasant (and warmer) alternative. When lake levels are low, a delightful beach is exposed along Europe Lake's northeast shore. This beach is part of Newport State Park, but it borders a handful of private cottages, so please respect their privacy. Access to this inland beach is best by canoe, but many parents wade the knee-deep water from the boat landing with their children on their shoulders, or with a picnic lunch in a day pack.

Exit Highway 42 north of Ellison Bay at Europe Bay Road. Turn left on Timberline Road to Europe Lake Lane and turn right (east) to the public landing at Europe Lake.

Sand Cove Beach

Sand Cove is one of those rare finds you stumble upon when you're hot, tired and ready for a dip. Located in Newport State Park, Sand Cove is often overlooked by beachcombers who are content to remain on the more accessible Europe Bay Beach. Those willing to take the half-mile hike to find Sand Cove will find a beautiful beach that is often empty, quiet and peaceful.

From lot 2 of Newport State Park (a state park vehicle admission sticker is required), head down the Newport Trail, but keep to the far left trail when it branches off.

BICYCLE TOURS

Whitefish Dunes Bicycle Tour *(10 miles)*

This tour follows inland Clark Lake on heavily wooded narrow roads tailor-made for bicycle travel. Swimming opportunities are available. In addition to

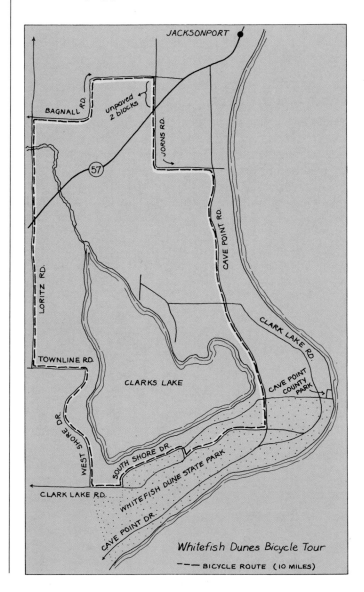

Whitefish Dunes Bicycle Tour

--- BICYCLE ROUTE (10 MILES)

following the Clark Lake shoreline, it also wanders by rural farms and fields.

After exiting Whitefish Dunes State Park, turn left on Cave Point Drive and follow this beautiful road through park land before taking the first right on unmarked South Shore Drive. At the first intersection turn left and head for the shore, where a public swimming beach awaits you. After taking a swim or enjoying the view, a left turn from the beach will take you back to Cave Point Drive. Continue on Cave Point Drive to West Shore Drive and turn right. Clark Lake will again be visible. Take West Shore Drive to Townline Road and turn left on Townline. The dead-end road here offers a small boat launch and a potential swimming location. From Townline take the first right onto Loritz Road. At sunset, deer may be seen in the fields off this road. Continue to Bagnall Road then turn right on Jorns Road (unpaved for two blocks), then cross Highway 57. Remain on Jorns Road to Cave Point Road and head back to Whitefish Dunes State Park.

Baileys Harbor Tour

This 23-mile tour winds through the Ridges Sanctuary to the historic Cana Island Lighthouse.

Beginning in downtown Baileys Harbor, head north through town to County Q. Pass Old County Q and turn right on Cana Island Road. At the first stop sign turn right, then bear left on paved roads to the Cana Island Lighthouse. A stone causeway provides foot access to Cana Island and its historic lighthouse, but plan your visit between 10:00 a.m. and 5:00 p.m. so you don't disturb the resident summer caretakers. Backtrack on Cana Island Road to County Q once again and turn right. Cross Highway 57 to Townline Road and turn left. Continue on Townline Road past German and Pioneer Roads. Once past Pioneer Road, Townline becomes Summach Road. Continue on Summach Road to the stop sign and turn right on

West Meadow Road. Continue past Cedar, bearing left at the stop sign, and you'll be on County F. County F will lead you back to Baileys Harbor.

BAILEYS HARBOR TOUR

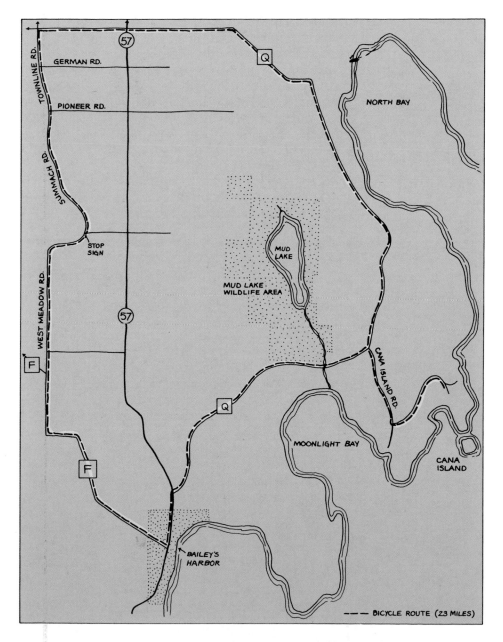

GERMAN RD.

PIONEER RD.

TOWNLINE RD.

SUMMACH RD.

WEST MEADOW RD.

57

57

Q

Q

F

F

STOP SIGN

NORTH BAY

MUD LAKE

MUD LAKE WILDLIFE AREA

CANA ISLAND RD.

MOONLIGHT BAY

CANA ISLAND

BAILEY'S HARBOR

– – – BICYCLE ROUTE (23 MILES)

Mink River Rolling Bicycle Tour

(9.5 miles)

MINK RIVER ROLLING BICYCLE TOUR

Tour country roads through orchards, rolling farmland and small woodlots in the town of Liberty Grove while following the path of the Mink River. The terrain is gentle, and although you won't see the river, the hidden preserve lies below you.

Begin at Mink River Road in the heart of Ellison Bay across from the Pioneer Store. This turn-of-the-century convenience market was built in 1900 and still retains its authentic charm and character. You'll be following Mink River Road to its conclusion at Waters End Road. Turn right on Waters End Road, pass over ZZ, then turn right on Old Stage Road. Pass over County Z to Highview and turn right. Take Highview to Lakeview. Turn left on Lakeview back to Mink River Road and turn left for the trip back.

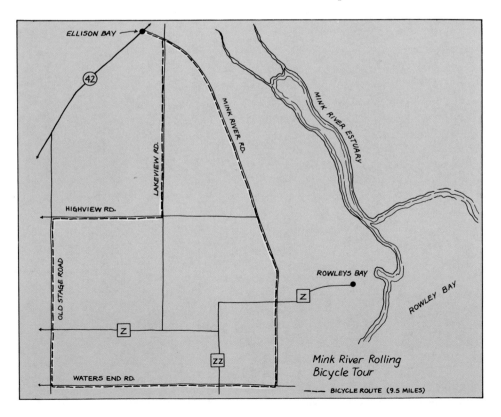

Mink River Rolling Bicycle Tour

- - - BICYCLE ROUTE (9.5 MILES)

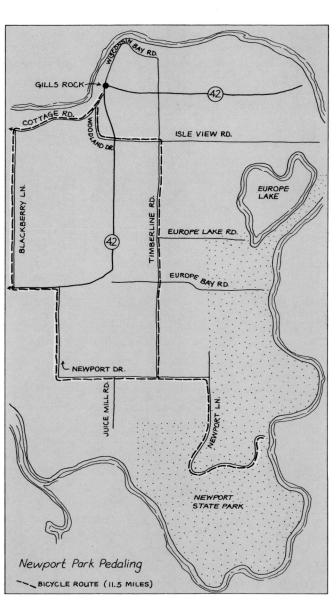

NEWPORT
PARK
PEDALING
BICYCLE
TOUR

Newport Park Pedaling

— — BICYCLE ROUTE (11.5 MILES)

Newport Park Pedaling *(11.5 miles)*

Tour the "top of the thumb" along Garrett Bay and Hedgehog Harbor through winding wooded hills, meadows, forest and farmland. Stop at the Gills Rock

153

ferry dock for a smoked fish lunch if you like, before heading back.

Beginning at the Newport State Park visitor contact station, head out of the park on South Newport Lane. Turn left on Newport Drive and continue straight past the sign marking the turn to Highway 42. You'll pass Juice Mill Lane as Newport Drive makes a sharp corner at the Schoenbrunn (Mink River) Nature Conservancy. Continue to Highway 42, and turn left on this busy road for two blocks, then turn right on Blackberry Lane. Continue on Blackberry up the two short hills and cruise down this beautiful bluff to Cottage Road. When you reach Highway 42, a left turn will take you to the Gills Rock Ferry. A right turn up Highway 42 continues your journey. Near the crest of Highway 42 turn left on Isle View Road and head three blocks to Timberline. Turn right on Timberline, then left on Newport Drive. Turn left on Newport Lane and head back to your starting point.

CANOE AND KAYAK ROUTES

Europe Lake

Europe Lake is a rare treasure. Much of the lake's eastern shoreline is part of Newport State Park, the exception being a family-owned resort just east of the boat landing. Its wild shoreline, sand bottom and limited development make Europe Lake a very appealing family canoe trip. When the water is low an excellent warm-water beach greets paddlers, but be sure you're on park property if you leave your canoe. Newport State Park has two campsites on Europe Lake accessible by canoe, but you can't leave your car overnight at the boat launch. That means someone has to move the car to the park and hike in. To get to the put-in, take Highway 42 north of Ellison Bay to Europe Bay Road. Take Europe Bay Road to Timberline Road, go left on Timberline to Europe Lake Road, and turn right to the boat launch. It takes about a half day to paddle around the lake, beginners and up can accomplish it, and summer is the best season.

Kangaroo Lake

Kangaroo Lake is a shallow, spring-fed, warm-water jewel best seen by canoe at sunset. You can spend an hour or a full day here admiring the woods, the cottages and the waterfowl. The lake reaches a maximum depth of 13 feet and covers 1,100 acres. Northern pike, walleye, largemouth bass and panfish constitute the fishery. Waterfowl use 340 acres of adjoining wetland for resting and nesting. This wetland is also accessible by canoe with a carry over the causeway that supports County E.

Kangaroo Lake occupies the depression left by glacial Lake Nippissing, and sand dunes now separate Kangaroo Lake and Lake Michigan. Heins Creek, a spring-fed stream in serious need of permanent protection, flows to Lake Michigan from a three-foot dam at the outlet from Kangaroo Lake. Much of the shoreline, including the island in the middle of Kangaroo Lake, is privately owned. Swimming, however, is pop-

KANGAROO LAKE

Kangaroo Lake takes its name from its unusual shape. This spring-fed lake is Door County's largest inland body of water. It contains walleye, bass, northern pike, perch and other panfish.

ular at the boat landing, and a sand bottom cushions the feet of those venturing to take a dip. Beginners and up can enjoy this trip spring, summer or fall.

The put-in is the boat landing off O'Brien Road. Exit Highway 57 north of Jacksonport at Logerquist Road. Turn right (east) on O'Brien Road to the public boat landing. Or, a canoe launch is possible from the causeway on County E that divides Kangaroo Lake. Exit Highway 57 south of Baileys Harbor west on County E to the causeway.

The author and his wife take a break while paddling Europe Lake.

Clark Lake

Whitefish Dunes State Park occupies a portion of the southeastern shore of Clark Lake and waterfowl appreciate the wooded wetland bordering this lake. With a maximum depth of 25 feet, Clark Lake is the deepest of the mainland lakes on the Door Peninsula (Mackaysee Lake on Chambers Island is a bit deeper)

and it supports an excellent fishery that includes walleye, northern pike, yellow perch and panfish.

The wind likes to whip up small waves on this wide
864-acre lake, but even beginners should have little
trouble getting to shore if the weather turns poor.
Clark Lake, like other inland lakes on the peninsula,
occupies a depression left by glacial Lake Nippissing.
The water is clear and the dunes separating Clark
Lake from Lake Michigan are part of Whitefish Dunes
State Park, insuring preservation of this geologic
wonder. An inlet stream called Logan Creek, which
also merits protection, enters Clark Lake from the
Lost Lake wetland northwest of here. Draining the
lake is Whitefish Bay Creek, a turquoise-colored
stream that flows in beautiful contrast to the dark
forest that lines its banks.

To get to the put-in, exit Highway 57 north of Sturgeon Bay at Clark Lake Road (en route to Whitefish
Dunes State Park).

Mud Lake

Mud Lake is a joy to experience by canoe. Undeveloped marsh, abundant waterfowl and a pristine natural setting provide a scenic treat for those who make
the effort to explore it.

The lake itself is just over one mile long and about
a half mile wide (155 acres), but it is surrounded by
750 acres of cedar, conifer and aspen that form its
wooded wetland border. Over 1,000 acres of this eco-
system have been designated the Mud Lake Scientific
Area, insuring its continued protection. The maximum depth here is five feet, but over half the lake is
less than three feet deep. Marl, a form of soft, spongy
soil, lines the lake floor, making a departure from
your boat regrettable.

Birding is a popular activity here since bald eagles,
ospreys, peregrine falcons, Cooper's hawks and red-
shouldered hawks are likely to use this area for feed-
ing and resting during migration.

This is a popular waterfowl hunting spot in the fall,
and canoeists are likely to find duck blinds as they
venture the one mile up Reibolt's Creek to Mud Lake.

CLARK LAKE

*Clark Lake is the
deepest of the in-
land lakes on the
Door County main-
land. This 868-acre
lake is home to
walleye, northern
pike, smallmouth
bass, perch, bluegill,
rockbass and carp.*

*The sandy area
of Clark Lake is ac-
tually a bay-mouth
bar separating this
inland lake from
Lake Michigan. As
the waters of an-
cient glacial Lake
Nippissing receded,
a bar of sand built
up across the front
of a shallow bay
and eventually iso-
lated what is now
Clark Lake.*

Current and wind can sometimes make travel a little rough on Reibolt's Creek, but when the rain is falling and the ducks are flying low, you may have hit just the perfect time for a Mud Lake getaway.

To get there, exit Highway 57 on County Q at Baileys Harbor. Launch where Reibolt's Creek enters Moonlight Bay and paddle upstream to Mud Lake. Public parking is available.

Cave Point Cruise

For sea kayakers, this is the best surfing beach on the peninsula. When whitecaps are breaking, wet or dry suits are recommended. Under calm seas, beginners will find the sand bottom and clear water inviting and nonthreatening. From the boat landing, paddlers heading north (left) will pass a series of summer homes before reaching Whitefish Dunes State Park. The tallest of these mountains of sand reaches 93 feet, and parking your boat on the beach for a hike is a great way to take a break.

Kayakers continuing on should be confident of their skills. Once Cave Point is rounded, waves deflecting from the cliffs become confused and unpredictable during even moderate weather conditions. However, this is an exceptionally beautiful area where Lake Michigan waves have eroded the limestone cliffs to form cave-like configurations. Rescue here is difficult and a capsize could be disastrous. If a shuttle vehicle is available, Schauer Town Park, off Cave Point Road north of Cave Point County Park, provides a convenient take-out point.

To get to the put-in on Whitefish Bay, exit Highway 57 north of Sturgeon Bay on County T in Valmy. Head east on County T until you see Lake Michigan and the boat landing. Navigation chart: NOAA #14910.

Mink River Estuary

This route, best undertaken by intermediates in a canoe or kayak, explores the beautiful Mink River Estuary. The Nature Conservancy says this is the last remaining high-quality estuary on Lake Michigan.

SEVASTOPOL SETTLER

The first permanent white settler of the present Township of Sevastopol was John Clark, who settled in the vicinity of Clark Lake in 1838.

Preserved for future generations, this 1,500-acre eco-system is unique. Bulrushes protect the wetlands from the waves and tidal effect of Lake Michigan. The wetlands contain plants threatened with extinction in Wisconsin. As many as 200 species of birds may use this area during migration. The waters provide a spawning ground for several kinds of fish, and fishing in season is excellent for both bass and Lake Michigan species.

To get there you can take County Z to the Wagon Trail Resort and use their landing on Rowleys Bay (fee charged). The put-in on Rowley Bay requires paddlers to follow the shoreline north. Wind is a problem for canoes here, as are waves once you leave the bay just before heading into the Mink River, but sea kayakers should have little trouble. To get to the alternate put-in, turn right on Newport Drive off Highway 42 north of Ellison Bay. Look for the sign at the corner where Newport Drive turns sharply left. That's the trail to the Mink River. The alternate put-in requires a very long portage (scout first), but avoids the open water of Lake Michigan. Navigation chart: NOAA #14909.

Europe Bay

A convenient put-in and a long pristine sand beach add up to a delightful day trip for beginning kayakers on this shoreline paddle. Europe Bay Beach is part of Newport State Park. Quiet observers may encounter wildlife along the shore since many animals make their homes in the rocky ledges as the beach gives way to rocky steps and cedar forest. Rounding the point, kayakers will find a day-use picnic area in this park. Backcountry campsites are available, but check with the ranger before setting up camp at Newport State Park. If it's July or August, make reservations in advance to assure a site.

To get to the put-in at Europe Bay Town Park, exit Highway 42 east of Ellison Bay at Europe Bay Road. (Follow the signs for Newport State Park.) Follow Europe Bay Road to its conclusion at the beach. Navigation chart: NOAA #14909.

WHITEFISH BAY CREEK

Whitefish Bay Creek is a one-mile-long outlet stream that drains Clark Lake, flowing through a cedar swamp into Lake Michigan. During high water, rainbow, brown and brook trout enter the creek.

CITIES, TOWNS AND VILLAGES

Baileys Harbor *(pop. 827)*

Baileys Harbor has long been a favorite retreat of mariners eager to take refuge in the shelter of its protected bay. Today, modern travelers find a different refuge amid the flowers, ferns and lapping waves.

The village takes its name from its founder, Captain Justin Bailey, a schooner pilot who discovered the harbor's safe haven during a fierce Lake Michigan gale in 1848. While waiting out the squall, Bailey explored the mainland, loading timber and building stone aboard his ship before continuing his journey south. Bailey's glowing report of this natural harbor prompted his employer, Alanson Sweet, to build a pier and open a stone quarry here in 1849, shipping timber and building stone south to Milwaukee. Mr. Sweet turned out to be quite a promoter, persuading the Wisconsin State Legislature to define the boundaries of the Door County and designate Baileys Harbor the county seat. Sweet attempted to change the name of the village to Gibraltar, but the change never took hold, and when Sturgeon Bay assumed the title of Door County seat in 1857, Captain Bailey regained his namesake.

Visitors to modern Baileys Harbor will find rugged shore, soggy swamp and virgin forest protected as a national landmark within the boundaries of Ridges Sanctuary, Toft Point Nature Conservancy and the Mud Lake Wildlife Area. It is here that the wild, untamed land that Captain Bailey found so inviting retains its natural appeal. Just southwest of Baileys Harbor, visitors will find Kangaroo Lake, the largest inland lake on the peninsula.

For information write: Baileys Harbor Information Center, Baileys Harbor, WI 54202; or phone: 414-839-2366. The library/town hall phone: 414-839-2210.

Boynton "Bjorklunden" Estate: Along the rocky Lake Michigan shore, Winifred and Donald Boynton built their famed "sanctuary of peace" in a wild setting on a 325-acre estate. Known as Bjorklunden, it includes a handcrafted Norwegian chapel based on a design

DOOR COUNTY SOILS

The soils and geology of the Door Peninsula present unique problems. Since the mantle of soil is so thin in most areas and the bedrock is in fractured layers, bacterial contamination of well water can occur. One faulty septic tank here can contaminate the drinking water of many wells.

Mrs. Boynton had seen beside a lake in Littlehammer, Norway. Open to the public during summer from 1 to 3 p.m. on weekends and Wednesdays, the Bjorklunden Chapel continues to inspire those who visit. The estate is currently administered by Lawrence University, Box 599, Appleton, WI 54912. A small ad-

A breakwater adds to the natural protection of Baileys Harbor.

mission is charged. Exit Highway 57 just south of Baileys Harbor at Lake Shore Drive toward Lake Michigan, then turn right on Chapel Lane.

Baileys Harbor Ridges Town Park: Immediately north of the village off Ridges Drive on Lake Michigan, this 30-acre park is adjacent to Ridges Sanctuary. There are picnic places and a great sand beach.

Anclam Town Park: This small park is located between Highway 57 and Lake Michigan in the village. There are picnic facilities, a small sand beach, and a boat ramp.

Baileys Harbor Fire Station Field: Adjacent to the village fire station, this 1.5-acre park offers tennis courts.

Baileys Harbor Recreation Field: Located off Summit Road west of the village with a baseball field and picnic facilities.

STOVEWOOD HOUSES

Houses constructed of stovewood set in mortar were commonly built in Door County during the late 19th century. They were essentially a poor man's building style, since a man could do all the work himself with materials located on his own farm.

Village of Jacksonport *(pop. 744)*

The village of Jacksonport lies halfway between the North Pole and the Equator, making it a pleasant crossroads for people to plan their future paths. Just south of the village lies Cave Point County Park. When Lake Michigan is venting its wrath here, you'll find geyser-like sprays erupting from the limestone ledges in a tribute to nature's forces.

The crashing waves are blamed for hurling at least two sailors to their deaths against the steep and unforgiving cliffs. In 1881, the schooner *D.A. Van Valkenburg,* laden with corn, was dashed against a reef near Cave Point. Three desperate crew members swam for shore. Only one was able to climb the rocky cliffs, emerging bruised and bleeding. The ship, meanwhile, burst under the pressure of the expanding corn in its hull. Its cargo washed ashore, providing feed for peninsula livestock.

Surrounding Cave Point is Whitefish Dunes State Park, another "must see" locale, and home to the largest sand dunes on the western shore of Lake Michigan. You'll need a state park vehicle sticker to

162

park here, but it's worth the price of admission when the sun is blazing and the waves are rolling in.

Jacksonport today is a close-knit community of farmers and merchants proud of their German lineage. They commemorate this heritage each August when antique farming equipment is exhibited at a local farm during the Thresheree. Another popular event is the annual Maifest Celebration over Memorial Day weekend when a cold brew and a hot bratwurst will have you dancing a polka.

Jacksonport Town Park: On County V east of the village, this park sports a baseball diamond.

Lyle Harter-Matter Sanctuary: The sanctuary is a 40-acre undeveloped wildlife area, completely wooded. It's located off Highway 57 north of Jacksonport.

Meridian County Park: Just north of Jacksonport, contiguous with Lyle Harter-Matter Sanctuary, this park is located halfway between the North Pole and the Equator. The park is heavily wooded with a wayside picnic area.

Lakeside Town Park: Located on the lakeshore off Highway 57 in the village, this park is the site of various festivities during the summer. It also has a nice sand beach.

Schauer Town Park: On Lake Michigan south of Jacksonport via Cave Point Road and Schauer Road, this small park (1.5 acres) provides a boat ramp.

STONE FENCES

Stone fences became boundaries as land was cleared, and serve the same purpose today. Composed of glacial rock, these fences tell a tale of hard labor and long days on peninsula farms.

ISLANDS

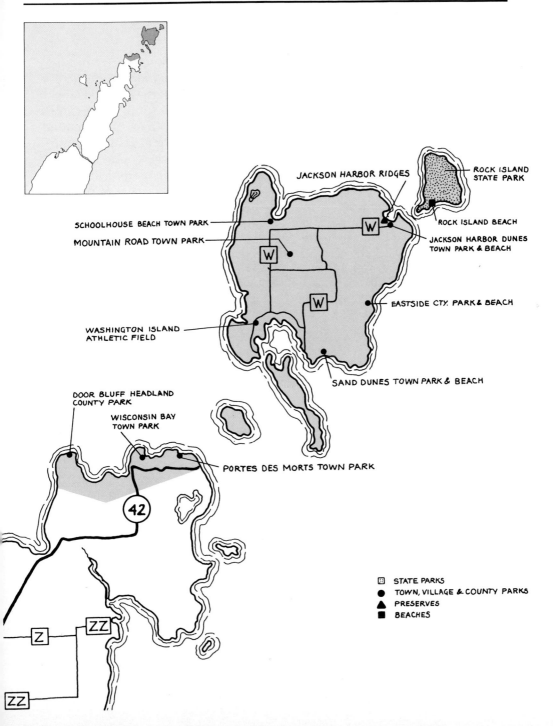

JACKSON HARBOR RIDGES

ROCK ISLAND STATE PARK

SCHOOLHOUSE BEACH TOWN PARK

MOUNTAIN ROAD TOWN PARK

ROCK ISLAND BEACH

JACKSON HARBOR DUNES TOWN PARK & BEACH

W

W

W

EASTSIDE CTY. PARK & BEACH

WASHINGTON ISLAND ATHLETIC FIELD

SAND DUNES TOWN PARK & BEACH

DOOR BLUFF HEADLAND COUNTY PARK

WISCONSIN BAY TOWN PARK

PORTES DES MORTS TOWN PARK

42

Z   ZZ

ZZ

◨ STATE PARKS
● TOWN, VILLAGE & COUNTY PARKS
▲ PRESERVES
■ BEACHES

Through the Windshield
AN OVERVIEW OF THE ISLANDS

The islands that dot the sparkling waters surrounding the Door Peninsula invite exploration. Called collectively the Grand Traverse Chain, these islands separate Wisconsin's Door Peninsula from Michigan's Garden Peninsula. Historically, Plum, Washington and Rock islands served as points of refuge for fur traders and voyageurs paddling the route between the Straits of Mackinac and the Mississippi River.

The Grand Traverse islands are glacially worn remnants of the ancient drainage separating the Green Bay and Lake Michigan basins. When bedrock is not directly exposed, it is covered by a thin layer of sand and silt that anchors the trees that shelter birds and wildlife. Of the eight islands and eight islets comprising the Grand Traverse Chain, about half are in Wisconsin and half are in Michigan.

A proposal to incorporate the five Wisconsin islands separating Green Bay from Lake Michigan into a state park or National Lakeshore has been discussed in the past but, unfortunately, the plan has no current initiative. The logical headquarters for such a park would be Washington Island. Beaches, bluffs, ridges and woodlands bring thousands of visitors to this 36-square-mile island each year. Most of the 75 miles of road are paved, and bringing a car or bicycle to the island allows you the freedom to explore at your leisure. Excursions to Washington Island begin at the tip of the Door Peninsula mainland with departures from either Gills Rock or the Northport Pier.

Sandwiched by Death's Door Bluff to the west and Table Bluff to the east, the harbor at Gills Rock provides a striking panorama. Early risers will find charter captains and commercial fishermen chugging out of the harbor in search of whitefish, trout and salmon. The car ferries that transport autos to Washington Island no longer dock here, but those wishing to tour the island by bicycle or guided tour can meet the 65-foot *Yankee Clipper* here from late May through mid-October (phone: 414-854-2972) or the

C. G. Richter run by a competing ferry service (phone: 414-847-2456). Competing tour "trains" also meet both the *Yankee Clipper* and the *C. G. Richter,* providing a narrated 90-minute tour of the island. Those wishing to conduct their own tours are welcome to bring their bicycles aboard, although bike or moped rentals are available on the island.

A third ship departing Gills Rock brings visitors to historic Fayette State Park on Michigan's Garden Peninsula. The *Island Clipper* sails twice weekly from late June through August, taking visitors past the entire Grand Traverse Island Chain, including Washington, Rock, St. Martin, Poverty, and Big and Little Summer islands. Reservations are recommended (phone: 414-854-2972). Sea kayakers have been known to take this route as well, but not with the same speed, comfort and safety offered by the *Island Clipper.* Once visitors complete the one hour, 45-minute crossing to Fayette, they dock for three hours at Snail Shell Harbor, where there are opportunities to tour the historic park, swim or enjoy a picnic lunch prior to the cruise back.

Continuing on Highway 42 you'll wind your way to the Northport Pier. You can credit landscape architect Jens Jenson for this scenic and unique drive. Instead of mowing down the forest to provide a perfect blacktop straightaway, Jenson convinced Door County officials to curve this wooded drive into a series of winding bends that seem to flow through the woods, becoming part of the landscape rather than altering it. Just prior to the ferry dock a town road leads to Porte des Morts Park. This town park preserves Table Bluff and also traces its conception to Jens Jenson. Jenson, a member of the Door County Parks Committee, envisioned preserving all of the county's bluffs as parkland. As you stand overlooking Washington and Plum islands the reason for his crusade becomes apparent.

Entering Northport you'll see a line forming to board the Washington Island car ferry on the far right of the roadway. These car ferries, which include the *Robert Nobel, Eyrarbakki* and *Washington,* serve as the island's lifeline, shuttling food, mail, equipment,

THE DEATH'S DOOR LEGEND

The six-mile passage separating Washington Island from the mainland takes its forboding name from Native American war parties who called this passage "Door to Death" because of the havoc the currents and weather could wreak upon their fragile canoes. French explorers shared the Indians' respect for this strait, translating the native term into Porte des Morts, or "Death's Door." Today, Coast Guard navigation aids guide both commercial and private vessels through the passage in safety and comfort.

visitors and residents across the Porte des Morts strait. During July and August the Washington Island Ferry Line offers more than 20 round trips daily, tapering off to five trips in September and only one round trip daily during January, February and March. Reservations are recommended during the winter months but unnecessary during summer (phone: 414-847-2546). You're welcome to bring your bike or kayak on board for an extra $1. Bringing your car across will set you back about $13 round trip plus the passenger fare of about $6 each. Those wishing to save the expense of personal transportation can take advantage of the Cherry Train Tour. A combination ferry and Cherry Train tour runs about $10 and includes a 90-minute narrated tour of the island in an open-air "train."

Boating across Death's Door Passage you'll see tiny Pilot Island to the east. For more than 40 years Pilot Island lived up to its name, providing a lighthouse that served as the only guide through these treacherous waters until a similar beacon was erected on Plum Island in 1886. Pilot Island, although federally owned, is privately leased. The 600-acre island immediately ahead is Plum Island, so named because it lies "plumb" in the middle of Death's Door Strait. The Coast Guard operates a manned station here, deriving its electrical power by underground cable from the mainland. This beautiful island has recently become overpopulated by whitetail deer, and their voracious appetites threaten island vegetation. Private vessels are welcome to dock here and visitation of the grounds, excluding the Coast Guard facilities, is permitted. There is an outstanding shallow harbor frequented by waterfowl on the northwest corner of the island, but overnight camping or boat mooring is not permitted.

Detroit Island looms ahead, guarding the entrance to Detroit Harbor and sheltering the ferry dock from vicious storms and swells. Detroit Island is privately owned and the independent folks that summer here depend on their own transportation to reach their homesteads. The island is not served by the Washington Island Electric Co-Op; residents depend on diesel fuel to generate electrical power.

DETROIT ISLAND

Peace-loving Potawatomi Indians would frequently hide on Detroit Island when bands of marauding tribes invaded their Rock Island territory.

Wheeling off the Washington Island Ferry you'll arrive on Pt. Lobdell Road. Bicycle rentals, tour train connections, shops and restaurants are located within walking distance of the landing. If you have a private vehicle or bicycle, this is where your island tour begins. Heading straight (north) on Pt. Lobdell Road you'll pass through a lovely forested grove with wide shoulders to accommodate bicyclists. Proceed 1.8 miles to Main Road and turn left. Main Road comes as close to a "downtown" as Washington Island has to offer. Development and attractions on the island are spread out, but clustered along Main Road is the post office, grocery store and island schools. Adjacent to the Washington Island School you'll find the best equipped indoor public recreation center on the

Rock Island is part of the Grand Traverse Island Chain. This archipelago stretches from Wisconsin's Door to Michigan's Delta peninsulas. St. Martin Island is visible in the distance.

Door Peninsula. Opened in 1988, the Washington Island Recreation Center boasts a four-lane swimming pool, whirlpool, locker room and exercise facility stocked with state-of-the-art equipment. This wonderful facility is the result of a one-million-dollar donation by John and Jane Mosling. The Moslings donated additional funds to maintain the facility and the result is striking. Visitors are charged a small fee for use of the center and hours vary depending on the season (phone: 414-847-2226).

If you wish to camp on Washington Island, you'll be sidetracking by turning right on Lake View Road just past the recreation center. Island Camping and Recreation is a 100-site private campground offering the only facilities where you can pitch a tent or wheel in an RV on Washington Island (phone: 414-847-2622, or 217-356-3226 during the off-season). Continuing your tour, following Main Road you'll pass the Maple Grove Golf Course. This par-35, nine-hole course is open to the public, offering clubs and carts for rent (phone: 414-847-2017). At the intersection of Jackson Harbor Road you'll find the Washington Island Art and Nature Center. Open daily except Saturdays from mid-June through August, including autumn Sundays, the Art and Nature Center offers exhibits and a short nature trail identifying island plants and environments. The center is a nonprofit, educational organization supported by donations, grants and memberships. A small admission fee is charged. Proceeding on Main Road you'll reach the intersection of Little Lake Road, which leads to Little Lake, and the Jacobsen Museum. Donated to Washington Island in memory of Jens Jacobsen, these scenic grounds and interesting museum recall island history in a cedar log building. The museum is open weekends from Memorial Day through mid-June; from mid-June daily through August; and weekends again through fall. A curator is on hand to answer your questions and offer advice. A small admission fee is charged. There is also carry-in boat access to Little Lake adjacent to the museum. Those without a canoe can walk out on the dock for a pleasant view of this ancient glacial lake.

FISHING MUSEUM

Located at Jackson Harbor, the Town Fishing Museum displays fishing artifacts and commercial processing equipment in a museum setting.

Backtracking on Little Lake Road you'll reach Jackson Harbor Road where you'll turn left (east). After a short jaunt down Jackson Harbor Road you'll reach a turnoff to Schoolhouse Beach. This town park offers a pebble beach and picnicking facilities in a beautiful setting overlooking Washington Harbor. The beach here is not well suited to young children since the drop-off is quite steep. Advanced swimmers, however, will enjoy taking advantage of the swim raft anchored offshore during the summer season.

Heading back down Jackson Harbor Road you'll discover the Washington Island Farm Museum. This free museum recalls the history of farming on the island. There is an original log building on the grounds stocked with hand tools used by the pioneers who carved out a living on this rugged island. The Farm Museum is open daily from Memorial Day weekend through October. Continuing on Jackson Harbor Road you'll pass Range Line Road before turning right on Mountain Road. Mountain Road leads to Mountain Park Lookout. A sturdy wooden staircase, donated by an islander and completed in 1989, climbs a steep hillside to an observation tower on top of the "mountain." The staircase eliminates the need to climb the steep trail that folks had to previously endure just to reach the observation tower, where another climb awaits. Your efforts will be rewarded when you reach the summit of the observation deck, which provides a stunning view of the island, Lake Michigan and points beyond.

Backtracking on Mountain Road and turning right on Jackson Harbor Road you'll pass Sievers Looms and School. This unique island business produces spinning and weaving looms in its woodworking shop. The Sievers School of Fiber Arts has more than 30 instructors who conduct both weekday and weekend classes during the summer and fall. Housing facilities are available for registered students (phone: 414-847-2264). Behind Sievers lies the rich and remote Coffey Swamp. This beautiful private wetland is inaccessible to the public but certainly merits permanent protection. Proceeding, Jackson Harbor Road leads to picturesque Jackson Harbor. The commercial

WASHINGTON ISLAND FACTS

Washington Island has about 550 year-round residents and about 3,000 summer residents. Nearly 78% of the island is owned by nonresidents. About 15 new homes are built each year.

fishing docks, boats and hard-working fishermen add to the distinct flavor of Jackson Harbor. This is where you can board the *Karfi* for the ten-minute trip to Rock Island State Park. No cars are allowed on this historic 900-acre preserve, but it's a wonderful place to spend an hour, a day or a week hiking, swimming, picnicking or camping. Just south of the state ferry dock you'll find Jackson Harbor Ridges. The Ridges, a state of Wisconsin Scientific Area, offers an outstanding example of beach, dune, boreal and shore meadow communities. A hiking trail crosses this town property and provides ample opportunity for careful exploration.

For the trip back to the car ferry dock, backtrack on Jackson Harbor Road to Deer Lane Road. This paved, wooded road is appropriately named since the white-tail population on the island is substantial and opportunities to spot deer, especially at sunset, are plentiful. From Deer Lane Road you'll be turning right on Town Line Road for a jaunt through the heart of Washington Island. At Range Line Road, turn left and you'll be heading back to Detroit Harbor Road where a right turn leads back to the ferry dock. If you're up for a swim, continue on Range Line Road past the marina to South Shore Drive. Just before the pavement turns to gravel you'll encounter Sand Dunes Town Park. The superb public beach here offers the best swimming opportunities on the island. Even if you're not up for a dip this park merits a visit, if only to sink your feet in sand and recall your island memories.

STATE PARKS

Rock Island State Park

This Lake Michigan island park is located off the northeast shore of Washington Island and is accessible by boat only. Commercial ferry service is available from Washington Island and private boat docking is allowed. Washington Island Ferry phone: 414-847-2425. Karfi (Rock Island) Ferry phone: 414-847-2425 or 414-847-2252. The address: Rock Island State Park, Washington Island, WI 54246. Phone: 414-847-2235.

FACILITIES:
There are 35 primitive campsites and five hike-in campsites. The island is equipped with pit toilets, drinking water and picnic facilities.

RECREATION:
There are hiking trails, nature trails, an excellent sand beach, an historic lighthouse and a cemetery to investigate. The park is open late spring through early fall.

For sheer beauty it's tough to beat Rock Island. Its isolation, unique geography and fascinating plant life make this peaceful island a place to cherish.

Located one mile from Washington Island, Rock Island is no picnic to get to. No doubt it was this isolation that attracted Rock Island's most famous former resident, Chester Thordarson. Thordarson, an Icelandic-born electrical genius, purchased most of the island in 1910. Using old-world craftsmanship, he proceeded to construct an outstanding great hall and a boathouse of native limestone. Both are currently maintained by the park and are open to visitors. The great hall conjures up images of Vikings and great maritime battles.

Perhaps of greater importance is what Thordarson chose not to develop. A conservationist himself, Thordarson left all but 30 acres of his island in its natural state. In 1964, the state of Wisconsin purchased Rock Island from the Thordarson estate and the task of developing the state park began.

CAMPING

State parks in Door County offer over 600 campsites, ranging from full-service units to backpacking sites. During the summer, reservations are recommended. Private campgrounds offer an additional 1,000-plus sites, so you'll always find a place to stake out your claim to Door County.

Today visitors use 40 primitive campsites, including five hike-in units. A glorious sand beach beckons body surfers, and over ten miles of hiking trails allow you to explore the park's natural treasures. Even if you plan only to picnic, make sure you take a hike. On the west side of the island you'll find huge cliffs that plunge down to Lake Michigan while on the eastern shore you'll find a half-mile-long sand beach.

Most visitors arrive via commercial ferry from Washington Island, although docking your private vessel at Rock Island is permitted.

If you're a camper, the most convenient (and expensive) method of getting to Rock Island requires that you take your car aboard the Washington Island Ferry from Northport. Once on Washington Island you must drive (see Washington Island map) to Jackson Harbor where you will board the *Karfi* for the ten-minute trip to Rock Island. Alternatives include paddling to Rock Island through Death's Door Passage, a difficult, challenging trip; pedaling from Detroit Harbor to Jackson Harbor—tough, but possible with the right camping gear; or snagging a taxi on Washington Island for the trip to Jackson Harbor. Regarding this last alternative, check with Vi's Taxi on Washington Island (414-847-2283). Vi has been known to shuttle campers, but call first.

Backpackers receive special attention on Rock Island with five campsites set aside to provide them with the peace and quiet they relish. Hikers will find room to roam with well-developed trails of various lengths that provide an interesting variety of flora and fauna. Day hikes are the most popular method of viewing the island, and a three-day weekend should allow you to hike most of the trails and still spend an afternoon on the beach. Budget extra time for crossing to the mainland, and bring adequate gear to weather a rainstorm since you'll be on your own once you start enjoying "the island life."

ISLANDS

ROCK ISLAND
STATE PARK

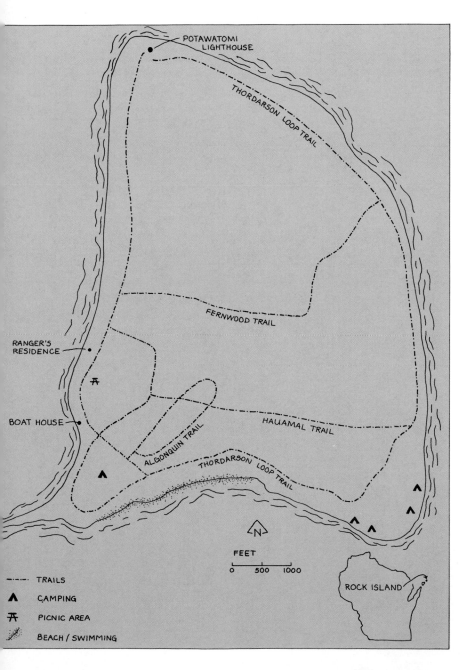

POTAWATOMI
LIGHTHOUSE

THORDARSON LOOP TRAIL

FERNWOOD TRAIL

RANGER'S
RESIDENCE

BOAT HOUSE

HAUAMAL TRAIL

ALGONQUIN TRAIL

THORDARSON LOOP TRAIL

N

FEET

0   500   1000

----- TRAILS

▲ CAMPING

⅄ PICNIC AREA

BEACH / SWIMMING

ROCK ISLAND

175

HIKING TRAILS

Thordarson Loop Trail: The Thordarson Loop (6.5 miles) is a great trail that takes hikers along a sand beach, over towering bluffs and along a rocky shore, presenting a sample of everything the island has to offer. This all-day hike is not to be rushed. You'll wish to pause for a picnic at the Potawatomi Lighthouse and take the steps down to the rocky shore. This trail can be hiked in either direction, but you may want to pack your swimsuit if you plan to return to the beach for a swim. Where the rocky ledges meet the sandy beach, be on the lookout for carvings on the small cliffs. They're hard to spot, but look closely and you'll find them.

Fernwood Trail: The 1.5-mile Fernwood Trail cuts the Thordarson Loop in half and provides a shortcut to the Potawatomi Lighthouse. An interesting stretch in its own right, the Fernwood Trail is aptly named. Quiet hikers on this trail may encounter white-tail deer near dusk and dawn, but since they live on an island they know the escape routes well.

Hauamal Trail: The Hauamal Trail (1.5 miles) begins at the picnic area and crosses the Algonquin Nature Trail, providing access to the furthest backpacking site on the island. This trail can also be combined with the Thordarson Trail to make a pleasant and interesting loop.

Algonquin Nature Trail: Even day visitors spending just an hour on Rock Island will have time to hike the one-mile Algonquin Nature Trail. This self-guided, one-way hike will both educate and entertain visitors to this island.

GLACIAL GLOSSARY

Moraine: deposits of soil and rock material carried by a glacier and deposited at its edges when the glacier melted.

Kettle: a depression formed by a block of glacial ice that was buried in debris and later melted.

Drumlin: streamlined, elongated hills composed of glacial till and paralleling the direction of flow of a glacier.

Esker: a long, sinuous ridge of stratified sand and gravel deposited by a stream that flowed through a tunnel at the base of a glacier.

(opposite page)

Sheer limestone cliffs rise one hundred feet above Lake Michigan on the northern shore of Rock Island State Park.

177

Grand Traverse Islands Park

A proposal to incorporate the chain of islands off the tip of Door County into parkland remains a grand idea stalled in the water by budget cuts and priority changes.

The islands—Plum, Pilot, Detroit, Washington, Hog and Rock—form the southern link in the Grand Traverse Islands Chain. Off Michigan's Garden Peninsula, the islands Little Summer, Summer, Poverty and St. Martin form the northern link. These islands are rich in history and stirring in beauty. This outstanding string of island pearls remains largely undeveloped, but without permanent protection this historic link between Wisconsin and Michigan remains in peril.

To date, only Rock and Washington Island accommodate overnight visitors. Plum Island, so named because it lies "plumb" in the middle of Death's Door Passage, is home to a manned Coast Guard station. In 1987, Wisconsin had an opportunity to lease the island from the Coast Guard. One of the provisions of that lease called for the state to construct a chain link fence around the Coast Guard facilities. Because the state failed to appropriate the $30,000 necessary to build the fence the Coast Guard withdrew its offer, further delaying plans for Grand Traverse Island State Park. Today, Plum Island remains open to day trippers wishing to moor their boats at the Coast Guard dock or slide their kayaks up the beach.

For 45 years the lighthouse on nearby Pilot Island was the only beacon mariners could rely on to negotiate safe passage through the Portes des Morts Strait. In 1886, a similar lighthouse was erected on Plum Island.

Detroit Island, another link in the Grand Traverse Chain, is a large, privately owned island with an interesting history. The first cabin built by white settlers in Door County stood (in 1834) near the northwest shore of this island. The Ottawa Indians who had lived there objected to the cabin since they had gardens and an ancestral burial grounds nearby. During a battle with these Indians one of the two builders of the cabin was killed and the other was rescued by a passing ship. The previous year, northern Michigan's famed "snowshoe priest," Bishop Frederic Baraga, visited the Ottawas and, at his urging, they built a bark chapel that he consecrated for their use.

Until about eighty years ago, Detroit Island was a storehouse of Indian relics. Burial mounds, well defined village sites, gardens, cairns and storage pits were found almost intact. All of this has been destroyed by souvenir hunters. Graves have been opened and plundered. Relics have been removed and burial grounds have been desecrated. Today, a handful of homesites stand along the shore but much of the island remains undeveloped.

Washington Island would serve as the logical headquarters for Grand Traverse Islands State Park. This island takes its name from a ship dispatched from Mackinac, Michigan, to establish a fort in Green Bay. The *Washington* was one of four schooners shuttling troops to the Door Peninsula in 1816. Arriving ahead of the other ships, the men of the *Washington* lay anchor off the island and named the harbor in which they were moored after their vessel. Although partially developed, Washington Island retains its enduring appeal. Boyer's Bluff, a spectacular wooded escarpment overlooking Lake Michigan, would make a fine addition to this proposed state park. The car ferries serving the island would provide a convenient link for further exploration of the Grand Traverse Chain.

The historic Potawatomi Lighthouse is found on the next link in the chain, Rock Island. Built in 1836, this lighthouse was the first navigational beacon operating in Wisconsin. During the 1850s and 1860s there was a school, church and even a doctor serving the island, which may have been the most populous settlement between Mackinac and Green Bay.

In 1910, Chicago industrialist Chester Thordarson, an Iceland native, purchased 661 acres on Rock Island for $5,735. In the late 1920s he built a magnificent boathouse and great hall that remain intact today. Thordarson proved to be an excellent steward of Rock Island and in 1964 the state of Wisconsin purchased his fine estate and the beautiful grounds surrounding it, establishing Rock Island State Park.

Perched above Rock Island, Potawatomi Lighthouse once served as the lonely outpost of a resident lighthouse keeper. Erected in 1836, this beacon is the oldest lighthouse in Wisconsin.

Crossing into Michigan you'll encounter St. Martin, Poverty, Summer and Little Summer islands completing the Grand Traverse Island Chain. These islands are privately owned, and rumblings of development and even a condominium project continue to surface.

The idea behind a Grand Traverse Islands State or National Park has been bandied about for over a decade. Now only strong public support and courageous government leaders can turn this unique concept into a public treasure.

TOWN, VILLAGE AND COUNTY PARKS.

Door Bluff Headlands County Park

(155 acres)

This is the largest county park on the Door Peninsula (155 acres), and one of the least visited. The headlands are actually bluffs that rise from the waters of Green Bay. It features interesting flora, rugged unmarked trails and steep topography, making it a challenge to explore. The park is reached off Highway 42 via Cottage Road to Garrett Bay Road to Door Bluff Road.

Wisconsin Bay Town Park *(.5 acres)*

This poorly marked town park offers a good view toward Washington Island. There is no beach and parking along the road is limited to only two cars.

Porte Des Morts Town Park *(2.5 acres)*

This Town of Liberty Grove park affords a great view of Washington and Plum islands. The site has two picnic tables and a grill. It is not well marked.

Washington Island Athletic Field

(4.4 acres)

Islanders take their summer baseball league very seriously, supporting them with zeal and enthusiasm. Chances are you'll get caught up in the action as well if you take in a game at the athletic field. Bleachers are provided and every seat in the house is a good one!

Sand Dunes Town Park *(4 acres)*

Access to the park is off South Shore Road about four miles east of the ferry dock. It has a great beach, and no crowds. Take the trail from the parking area up the hillside to the sand dunes and enjoy yourself.

ISLAND BASEBALL

Island residents are proud of their baseball team, and cheering the team on is a favorite summer event.

181

Eastside County Park *(5.2 acres)*

A secluded sand beach, picnic tables and a pair of fire rings make this park worth the trip down the gravel road to get there. The park takes its name from its location—on the eastern side of Washington Island.

Jackson Harbor Dunes Town Park *(31.5 acres)*

The docking facilities at Jackson Harbor Park are home port to many of the island's commercial fishing operations, and this pier has a distinctive "salty" appeal. The sand beach is an inviting place to swim. Changing houses are available. A hiking trail crossing the adjacent sand dunes provides an outstanding natural classroom. The Nature Conservancy has been instrumental in protecting this area and recently a critical parcel has been added to this preserve (listed separately).

Schoolhouse Beach Town Park *(34 acres)*

This town park once served as the Washington Island campground, but now the smooth stone beach and beautiful view of Washington Harbor are its chief attractions. A swimming raft is anchored offshore but this beach is best utilized by experienced swimmers since the water becomes quite deep just offshore. The park is well marked off Jackson Harbor Road.

Mountain Road Town Park *(5 acres)*

A heart-pounding climb provides an excellent view of Washington Island from an observation tower atop the mountain that gives this park its name. A newly constructed staircase leads to an observation tower. This climb is not for the faint of heart, but those with stamina will be rewarded with a fine vista.

PRESERVES

Jackson Harbor Ridges

Located at Jackson Harbor on Washington Island. Owned by the town of Washington Island and managed by the Washington Island Natural Area Board, this preserve was protected with assistance from the Nature Conservancy. For more information write: Arni Richter, Washington Island, WI 54246. Phone: 414-847-2296.

RECREATION:
The park is open year-round for hiking, nature study and photography.

This unique preserve encompasses an incredible diversity of natural communities including lake dunes and ridges, limestone sand flats and conifer forest. The Nature Conservancy says the rare combination of ecosystems that are part of Jackson Harbor Ridges makes this the only beach of its kind known on the islands surrounding the Door Peninsula.

Cool, moist Lake Michigan breezes create a climate here conducive to the growth of rare plant species such as dwarf lake iris and arctic primrose. The beach gives way to a stand of pine trees and the site provides an outstanding view of Jackson Harbor. The wet upland forest is home to white cedar, fir and spruce trees. The Nature Conservancy says hikers also should be on the lookout for other plant species including shrubby St. John's wort, dune goldenrod and prairie sandreed along the ridges and dunes of Jackson Harbor.

Protection of Jackson Harbor Ridges began in 1972. The town of Washington Island, assisted by the Nature Conservancy, purchased 42 acres that year along the southern boundary of Jackson Harbor, creating a public nature preserve. In 1988, the Nature Conservancy added a 43-acre tract adjacent to the original parcel.

Today, Jackson Harbor Ridges is an 85-acre natural area with 27 acres devoted to "biological and wildlife

Twisted cedar roots cling precariously to a limestone cliff at Death's Door Park near Gills Rock.

study, photography and 'careful walking,' " so plan your low-impact visit accordingly.

After arriving at Detroit Harbor aboard the Washington Island Ferry, head north along County W to Jackson Harbor. Turn off at Rock Island Road to Sunrise Road. Turn left at Sunrise Road and watch for the preserve just as the road bends right (east). Jackson Harbor Ridges is bordered by Town of Washington Island parkland to the west, but private property to the east along Sunrise Road. Please avoid trespassing.

184

BEACHES

Washington Island Sand Dunes

Deep, enchanting sand dunes cushion beach blankets on Washington Island's public beach. Because Washington Island is frequently fanned by cool Lake Michigan winds, the dunes provide a warm place to escape the breeze and absorb the heat of the sand on a sunny summer day. The island dunes also provide a grand view of Detroit Island and Lake Michigan.

From Detroit Harbor, take County W briefly to Detroit Harbor Road and turn right (east). Follow Detroit Harbor Road to County W until it becomes South Shore Drive about one mile to Washington Island Sand Dunes.

Eastside County Park Beach

The sand beach at Eastside County Park provides a nice place to beat the heat when other island beaches are beginning to get a little crowded. You'll have to travel across a gravel road to get to this one.

Jackson Harbor Beach

With Rock Island before you and the Jackson Harbor Dunes behind you it's tough to imagine a better location from which to enjoy a sunny day. Changing stations are available and the beach is a great place to absorb the rays while you wait to board the *Karfi* for a trip to Rock Island.

Schoolhouse Beach

The smooth pebble stones at Schoolhouse Beach are no substitute for sand, but the grand view of Washington Harbor and the swimming raft still attract plenty of visitors. This beach is not well suited for small children or poor swimmers, but those with experience in water will enjoy a visit.

PRIVATE PROPERTY
Most of the land on Washington Island is held in private ownership. Residents respect their privacy and hope you will too.

A pair of Rock Island sun lovers find room to relax during a mid July retreat.

Rock Island Beach

This beach conjures up images of Robinson Crusoe. Its magnificent isolation insures plenty of comfort. Sand dunes form a stunning backdrop and waves often provide opportunities for body surfing. A frequent breeze can chill a swimmer, but in July it's tough to resist frolicking in the surf.

Take the Washington Island Ferry from the Northport dock to Detroit Harbor. Drive, bike, hitchhike or take an island taxi to Jackson Harbor. Board the passenger ferry *Karfi* for the ten-minute crossing to Rock Island. The beach is on the southeast side of the island, adjacent to the campsites.

186

BICYCLE TOURS

Washington Island Wheeling

(15 miles, 21 miles with sidetracks)

This tour follows paved roads through the heart of the island. There are opportunities to swim, sightsee and picnic as you travel from Detroit Harbor to Jackson Harbor amid the forests and fields of Washington Island.

Begin the tour as you depart the Washington Island ferry. Heading up Point Lobdell Road you'll enjoy the wide shoulders and scenic forest as you make your way the 1.8 miles to the intersection with Main Road. Turn left on Main Road and you'll be pedaling into the island's "downtown" district, passing the island school, grocery store and community center. When you reach the Island Art and Nature Center at Jackson Harbor Road, you can either take the 3.6-mile round-trip sidetrack to Little Lake and the Jacobsen Museum or turn right on Jackson Harbor Road. A short jaunt off Jackson Harbor Road leads to Schoolhouse Beach. The smooth pebble beach here provides swimming opportunities and the view of Washington Harbor is worth the side trip even if you don't plan to take a dip. Continuing you'll pass the Washington Island Farm Museum before you reach the intersection with Mountain Road. A two-mile round-trip sidetrack down Mountain Road takes you to Mountain Lookout Town Park. A wooden staircase leads to an observation tower providing a sweeping view of the surrounding countryside. Backtrack to Jackson Harbor Road and continue past Sievers Looms and School to Jackson Harbor. You can catch the *Karfi* to Rock Island if you wish or explore the dunes and boreal forest of Jackson Harbor Ridges. Backtrack on Jackson Harbor Road to Deer Lane Road and turn left. This narrow road is tailor-made for bicycling. Continue to Lakeview Road and turn right. Proceed to Range Line Road and turn left. Range Line Road intersects with Detroit Harbor Road which will intersect with Point Lobdell Road for the trip back to

WASHINGTON ISLAND WHEELING BICYCLE TOUR

the ferry dock. If you've got a little extra energy and are up for a swim, continue straight on Range Line Road past Aznoe Road and turn left on South Shore Drive. South Shore Drive is paved up to Sand Dunes Public Beach. Here you'll find the finest swimming the island has to offer.

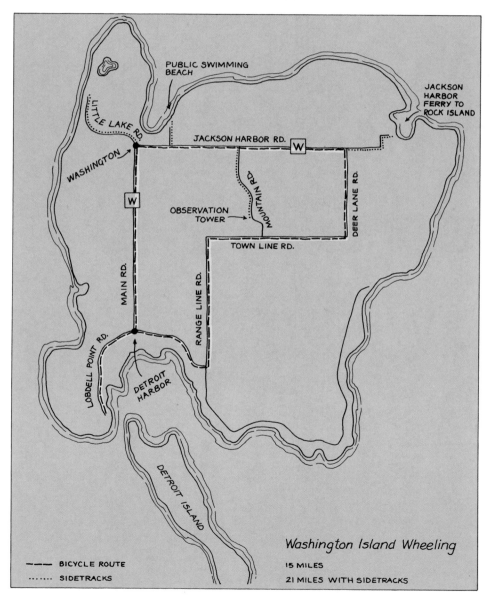

PUBLIC SWIMMING BEACH

JACKSON HARBOR FERRY TO ROCK ISLAND

LITTLE LAKE RD.

WASHINGTON

JACKSON HARBOR RD.

W

MOUNTAIN RD.

OBSERVATION TOWER

DEER LANE RD.

W

MAIN RD.

TOWN LINE RD.

RANGE LINE RD.

LOBDELL POINT RD.

DETROIT HARBOR

DETROIT ISLAND

Washington Island Wheeling

— — BICYCLE ROUTE
······· SIDETRACKS

15 MILES
21 MILES WITH SIDETRACKS

CANOE AND KAYAK ROUTES

Death's Door Passage

Death's Door translates from the French name for this strait, "Porte des Morts." Passage today can be an uneventful cruise aboard the Washington Island Ferry, or a major expedition undertaken by expert sea kayakers. Even in promising weather, this seven-mile crossing should not be taken lightly. Currents are unpredictable in the passage and swells, invisible from shore, often become steep and threatening. Plum Island in the middle of Death's Door can provide needed refuge during an emergency, but camping is prohibited. A manned Coast Guard station on the island will provide reassurance for paddlers as will the sight of the car ferry chugging through the strait. Rock Island State Park, off Washington Island's northeast shore, is a favorite destination of sea kayakers, making for a long day of paddling. Only a handful of paddlers successfully challenge this crossing each summer, but those who do enjoy rewards few others will ever know.

To get to the put-in at the Northport Dock, take Highway 42 east of Gills Rock to the tip of the peninsula. Navigation chart: NOAA #14909.

Little Lake

Access: Carry-in public access to Little Lake is available next to the Jacobsen Museum, reached via Main and Little Lake roads.

You'll be glad you car-topped your canoe for the ferry ride trip to Washington Island once you discover 24-acre Little Lake. Little Lake is a crystal-clear pool located just a short way from Lake Michigan. Due to its limited development, you're likely to startle ducks, geese and herons as you paddle the marshy northwestern shoreline. The lake occupies a shallow bowl carved by glacial action and is separated from Lake Michigan by a cobblestone ridge. At normal water levels, Little Lake is a full three feet higher than Lake Michigan. The lake reaches a maximum depth

of five feet and because of winterkill, fishing is poor. Nevertheless, its near-pristine shoreline and clear waters combine to make lily dipping in Little Lake a simple pleasure. Even though you will be sorely tempted to do so, please avoid landing on the wooded shore. This is private property and the owners appreciate their privacy.

Rock Island Reefs

Kayakers willing to endure the expense of car topping their boats aboard the Washington Island Ferry can cross the dangerous Porte des Morts in comfort, safety and convenience. After arriving at Detroit Harbor, drive to Jackson Harbor where you'll find the *Karfi* loading passengers for the ten-minute ferry ride to Rock Island. The captain of the *Karfi* can advise kayakers of the conditions for the crossing to Rock Island, and, if necessary, shuttle your gear for a fee. Keeping the *Karfi* in sight will boost your confidence as you make your way to Rock Island. Before setting up camp on Rock Island, you'll need to secure a permit from the ranger. Once on the island, paddling opportunities for circumnavigation are limitless, but beware of the weather. In this portion of the peninsula storms roll in quickly and can strike with a vengeance. During periods of fair weather, though, this is a lovely, blue open-water crossing for kayakers with intermediate skills and up. Navigation chart: NOAA #14909.

To get to the put-in at Jackson Harbor, leave the ferry dock on Washington Island by Point Lobdell Road. Turn left on Main Road to Jackson Harbor Road and turn right.

(opposite page)
Rock Island is a popular destination for experienced sea kayakers.

CITIES, TOWNS AND VILLAGES

Washington Island *(pop. 550)*

Washington Island rises from Lake Michigan using regal bluffs, stunning sand dunes and shady swamps to cast a magical spell on all who visit. The folks who call it home like to boast they live "north of the tension line," and visitors watching the ferry leave them behind are inclined to agree.

Today, getting to Washington Island is both safe and convenient aboard diesel-powered steel ships that routinely ply the Porte des Morts Strait. One hundred years ago the opposite was true. In fact, between 1872 and 1889 a lighthouse keeper on Pilot Island recorded an average of two shipwrecks a week in this area. Winter crossings have also taken their toll. In March of 1935, before the luxury of year-round ferry service, six young islanders returning by vehicle from the mainland put their trust in the winter ice. It was to be their final trip since the frozen strait had opened, sealing their fate.

Early Indian inhabitants of Washington Island not only feared the passage to the mainland, but also depended on it for protection from ambush by enemies. Archaeological explorations of the island have uncovered evidence of these early settlements and a window to their past.

The appeal of Washington Island lies in not only its isolation, but also its tempered climate. Influenced by the blue waters that surround it, the island remains cooler in the summer and warmer in the winter than its midwestern neighbors.

Outstanding fisheries drew the island's first white settlers and continue to attract tourists eager to battle salmon or trout aboard fishing charters that troll the island's 26 miles of shoreline. Door Peninsula historian Hjalmar Holand, never one to pass up a story even if it does sound a little fishy, tells of a 70-pound trout caught off Rock Island in 1860. Holand follows this tale with reports of a single fisherman netting 220 trout in just two days.

STRICT ZONING

Washington Island was the first township in Door County to adopt a strict zoning code. This has protected the island from overdevelopment and assured that its scenic values will remain for future generations.

Woodcutters followed fishermen to Washington Island, finding that steamships laden with fish required fuel for the trip south. These hearty woodsmen were mostly Norwegians, Danes and Icelanders who began hammering out a living from the native timber. The influence of these native Scandinavians remains, and today the island is home to the oldest heritage of Icelandic ancestry in the United States.

Washington Islanders have always felt deeply attached to both their land and their neighbors. Environmental awareness has led to the creation of excellent parks, beaches and nature preserves with strict zoning laws assuring planned development. Community pride and cohesion is evident among local residents who support their summer baseball team with all the zest and loyalty of a major-league franchise. Many visitors choose to retire here, enjoying the safe, friendly atmosphere after discovering, as you may, that Washington Island is a great place to visit, but they'd rather live here.

Getting to Washington Island: Most visitors arrive aboard the Washington Island Ferry from Northport or Gills Rock. Some bring their private vessels and dock at either Detroit or Jackson harbors. A handful arrive by kayak, usually en route to Rock Island. And, the island also has a class A airport accommodating private airplanes.

Many visitors bring their own vehicles aboard the car ferry, enjoying the freedom while enduring the expense of personal transportation. Alternatives include taking an island tour train or renting a moped or a bicycle. Personal guided tours are also available.

Art and Nature Center: The center at the corner of Main and Jackson Harbor roads offers classes in art and nature. It's an excellent orientation spot for visitors. The center is open from the third week in June through September. A small admission is charged.

Washington Island Farm Museum: The museum offers a look at the history of farming on Washington Island. It's open from late May through October and admission is free.

ISLAND FESTIVITIES

Fireworks on the Fourth of July

Fly-in fish boil on the third Sunday in July

Scandinavian Festival on the first weekend in August

Island Fair on the third Thursday in August

Fireman's Ball on the second Saturday in August

Fall Ball and Harvest Dinner on the second Saturday in October summer.

Sievers School of Fiber Arts: Weekend and week-long classes in spinning and weaving are offered here. The school is located on Jackson Harbor Road and offers dormitory-style lodging for students.

Library: The library is located off Lake View Road in the Community Center.

Jacobsen Museum: Located on the south shore of Little Lake, six miles from the ferry dock on the northwest corner of the island, the museum has a fine collection of natural and historic artifacts. It's open weekends from Memorial Day through mid-June, then daily through the summer. It is a great source of tourist information late in the season before it closes in mid-October.

Washington Island Chamber of Commerce: The address: Box 80, Washington Island, WI 54246; phone: 414-847-2225.

Sand Dunes Town Park: Access to the park is off South Shore Road about four miles east of the ferry dock. It has a great beach, and no crowds. Take the trail from the parking area up the hillside to the sand dunes and enjoy yourself. Four acres.

Schoolhouse Beach Town Park: This 34-acre park offers a marked swimming area with a raft for advanced swimmers. It's located five miles from the ferry dock on Washington Harbor, off Cemetery Road via Main and Jackson Harbor roads.

Eastside County Park: There's a great view of Hog Island, a national wildlife refuge for nesting herons, gulls and shorebirds, as well as picnic facilities here. Follow Lakeview Road to Lake Michigan.

Jackson Harbor Ridges: This nature preserve is not to be missed. The ridges here are actually sand dunes separated by low-lying depressions called swales. Endangered plants cling to life here, so plan a low-impact visit.

Mountain Road Town Park: Access to this five-acre park is off Mountain Road via Main and Jackson Harbor roads. A steep trail takes visitors to the summit of this 160-foot mountain. An observation deck on top puts you above the trees for an island view.

ISLAND DOCTOR

Washington Island has a resident doctor who keeps regular hours at the Washington Island Clinic. She is always on call for emergencies and urgent care. The island also has a team of trained Emergency Medical Technicians available for medical emergencies.

Washington Island Sand Dunes: Deep, enchanting sand dunes cushion beach blankets on Washington Island's public beach. Because Washington Island is frequently fanned by cool Lake Michigan winds, the dunes provide a warm place to escape the breeze and absorb the heat of the sand on a sunny summer day. The island dunes also provide a grand view of Detroit Island and Lake Michigan.

From Detroit Harbor, take County W briefly to Detroit Harbor Road and turn right (east). Follow Detroit Harbor Road to County W until it becomes South Shore Drive about one mile to Washington Island Sand Dunes.

Washington Island Ferry Service

Gills Rock and Northport, both at the tip of the peninsula, are the two locations from which to launch your exploration of Washington Island. The two docks are served by competing commercial ferry operations. If you plan to bring your car to the island, you'll be departing from Northport, two miles east of Gills Rock at the end of Highway 42. If you plan to make the trip just to enjoy the scenery, or if you're bringing your bike for an island tour, you can save the expense of shuttling your car and board at either Gills Rock or Northport.

The trip from Gills Rock takes passengers aboard the *Yankee Clipper*. This 149-passenger ship, operated by Voight Marine Services, began operations in 1971. Captain Voight offers up to five round trips daily and affords a narrated crossing through Death's Door Passage from the last week in May through mid-October. Cost is about $12 round-trip and the *Yankee Clipper* doesn't charge for bicycles. You can combine this adventure with a guided tour of Washington Island aboard the Viking "Train" for an additional charge. For current fees and departure information phone: 414-847-2546.

A second vessel in the Voight fleet, the *Island Clipper*, sails twice weekly from Gills Rock to Fayette State Park on Michigan's Garden Peninsula. This all day, 34-mile trip takes one hour and 45 minutes each way and passes the historic Grand Traverse Island

Chain before docking in Snail Harbor. During the three-hour stop at Fayette there are opportunities to tour the restored historic town site, swim and picnic. Sea kayakers might be able to make arrangements to be picked up at Fayette if they're willing to challenge the spectacular crossing from Wisconsin to Michigan. The boat sails from late June through August and reservations are recommended, phone: 414-854-2972.

If you plan to bring your car to Washington Island, you'll be departing from the Northport Dock aboard ferries owned and operated by the Washington Island Ferry Service. Northport affords an ice-free passage to Washington Island in winter and shortens the trip from 45 to about 30 minutes in summer. Northport's summer residents protested moving the bulk of traffic from Gills Rock to this sleepy dock but were defeated by arguments made in the name of safety by the Washington Island Ferry Line.

The car ferries serving Washington Island run year-round, regardless of weather. Occasionally, severe winds leave travelers stranded, but this is rare. Those prone to seasickness should take the necessary precautions since the trip can sometimes be a roller-coaster ride. Frequency of service depends upon the season. In winter when only one round trip is scheduled daily, automobile reservations are advisable. During July and August more than 20 round trips daily are offered, with weekend evening service available from mid-May through mid-August. If you plan to bring your car, you'll pay about $13 round-trip for the vehicle plus an additional $6 per person round-trip. Bicycles and kayaks are carried for $1 each. Boat trailers, recreational vehicles and campers are permitted to board for an additional fee. You must be in line at least ten minutes early. For current fees and precise departure information phone: 414-847-2546.

Since purchasing the Washington Island Ferry Line in 1940, the late Carl G. Richter, and most recently his son, Arni, have made several additions to the ferry fleet. At the time of purchase, two vessels, the *Welcome* and the *North Shore*, provided daily service from Ellison Bay and later Gills Rock to Washington Island. The first addition to the fleet was an all-steel

ship, christened the *Griffin* in honor of the first sailing ship to ply the Great Lakes. Fortunately, the Washington Island Ferry Line *Griffin* didn't suffer the same fame as La Salle's vessel, which sailed from the island and vanished. The second ship added to the fleet was named the *C. G. Richter* in honor of the senior ferry line owner. The original two ships were sold for service elsewhere and the fleet continued to expand. The *Voyageur* was built in 1960 and named in honor of French fur traders who paddled the inland seas surrounding Door County. The *Eyrarbakki* joined the fleet in 1970 and was named for the Icelandic town from which the first Scandanavian settlers departed to settle Washington Island.

The latest addition to the Washington Island Ferry Line was the *Robert Noble*. This 87-foot ship was built in Sturgeon Bay and named in honor of the first man to offer ferry service across the Sturgeon Bay shipping canal.

While the Washington Island Ferry Line is best known for serving residents and visitors of the island for which it is named, it has also come to the aid of stranded Sturgeon Bay residents. During November 1960, the Swedish ship *Carlsholm* rammed the city's downtown bridge. At the time, only a single bridge served Sturgeon Bay residents, and the accident threatened to isolate both sides of the city. Ferry line owner Arni Richter summoned his crews and brought the *Voyageur* and the *C. G. Richter* to Sturgeon Bay, running a 24-hour-a-day schedule for ten days until a temporary bridge was erected.

(opposite page)
Resident waterfowl find safe haven at Gills Rock.

Gills Rock *(pop. 75)*

Gills Rock is best seen from the Washington Island Ferry as it approaches Garrett Bay and Hedgehog Harbor at the base of this New England–style village. Flanked by Death's Door Bluff to the west and Table Bluff to the east, Gills Rock has long been a haven for commercial fishermen earning their living amid the white-crested waves of Lake Michigan.

Porcupines are credited with naming Hedgehog Harbor. The story goes that Gills Rock pioneer Allen Bradley christened the harbor after discovering that his neighbor's boat had been gnawed by porcupines as it rested at Gills Rock over the winter.

Gills Rock today is considerably less chaotic than it was when automobiles waited in line to board the Washington Island Ferry. The end of the dock is a perfect place to enjoy a smoked fish snack if you can convince the gulls to find their own lunch. Winter is peaceful at this serene village, and as the waves crash and the ice builds on the dock, it's easy to forget it's time for the journey home.

Door County Maritime Museum: The museum is in Gills Rock at Wisconsin Bay Road and is open from Memorial Day to Labor Day. It features exhibits of marine artifacts and commercial fishing equipment.

Porte des Morts Town Park: There's a great view across Death's Door Passage from this small park (2.5 acres). There are also picnic facilities. The park is reached east of Gills Rock off Park Drive.

Gills Rock Memorial Park: This park features a ballpark, museum and picnic facilities. It's located in the village off Wisconsin Bay Road.

Gills Rock Advancement Association: Write to them at Gills Rock, WI 54210.

EXPLORING SHIPWRECKS

There are about 120 shipwrecks surrounding Door County. Over fifty of these ships went down in the waters surrounding Washington and Rock islands. In fact, the area is known as the graveyard of the Great Lakes. Scuba divers frequently dive these wrecks, occasionally making new discoveries. Shipwreck sites are protected and removing artifacts is not permitted.

Northport *(pop. 75)*

A narrow, winding road through a forest grove brings visitors to the Northport Pier. Once a sleepy shoreside community of summer residents, Northport came to life when the Washington Island Ferry Line switched its operations from Gills Rock to the Northport Pier. Northport was the traditional landing site during the winter months and provided an alternative summer landing during strong northerly winds.

Improvements at the landing began in 1982, against the vocal protests of nearby property owners. A long court battle ensued and it wasn't until several years later that the courts ruled in favor of the ferry line allowing added development, including the addition of a restaurant at the landing. While local property owners were stunned by the decision, Washington Islanders were delighted. Not only does Northport provide an ice-free port in winter, it also cuts the crossing time to the island from 45 minutes to about 30 minutes. Owners of the Washington Island Ferry Line received no government support to defray the $500,000 price tag of improvements at the pier. But summer residents, still bitter over the court decision to expand the landing, consider the loss of their peace and quiet priceless.

EPILOGUE:
THE FUTURE

The legacy of the Door Peninsula is one of wild and beautiful shores, towering limestone cliffs and deep, aromatic forests. Its heritage is one of inquisitive explorers, self-reliant settlers and steadfast preservationists.

Over the years, ax has given way to bulldozer, meadows to condominiums and dirt roads to paved highways. Some call it progress; others, exploitation. Somewhere in between lies a delicate balance.

Door County's groundwater remains its most valuable and fragile natural resource. Land development, agriculture, road construction and urban sprawl threaten this water table. Left exposed by shallow soil and a limestone backbone, this resource is vulnerable to pesticide pollution, soil erosion and septic tank pollution.

Many critical ecosystems depend on this water for their continued existence. These ecosystems merit special attention for both their aesthetic value and irreplaceable natural heritage. Dunes Lake Marsh north of Sturgeon Bay provides a striking example of this environment. This extensive, wild wetland is mostly swamp, marsh or ridge-swale topography. Maple Creek and its associated wetlands feed the lake, providing an important undisturbed home to wildlife and waterfowl. Shivering Sands Creek drains the marsh.

Also nearby is an area known as Cranberry Marsh. It consists of an extensive deep-water swamp and shallow wilderness lake. An upland forest separates the marsh from Lake Michigan. Combined, this large and complex ecosystem is perhaps the finest undeveloped roadless area on the peninsula. Its proximity to Whitefish Dunes State Park makes it a logical addition to this preserve. To date, its private owners have resisted developing the tract, but without permanent protection its unique character remains in jeopardy.

(opposite page)

Giant sand dunes, cloaked in vegetation, reach heights of nearly one hundred feet at Whitefish Dunes State Park.

Other wetlands, including Coffey Swamp, a remote sedge bog on the north shore of Washington Island, the marshes on both ends of Kangaroo Lake, and the Lost Lake drainage area also provide critical habitat for insects, amphibians and waterfowl. These wetlands add diversity to this charming land. They also recharge the water table, supplying food and shelter to peninsula wildlife.

Creeks, streams and springs add to the peninsula's diverse fishery. Brook trout were once found in Logan, Hidden Spring, Keyes, Lilly Bay, Ephraim and Three Springs creeks. Today many of these creeks have been choked by road construction or drained for land development. Woodard, Stoney, Shivering Sands, Heins and Bear creeks support smelt runs. Game fish also spawn in these creeks and adjacent wetlands. It is up to us to assure that this natural cycle continues.

Early settlers were drawn to the Door Peninsula by its vast forests. Modern travelers arrive seeking the same commodity. Today about 8,000 acres of forest remain preserved in Door County parklands. The remaining woods are privately owned by commercial interests, farmers and recreational landowners. Unlike forests in some northern Wisconsin counties, the worth of Door Peninsula timber is measured not by its market price, but by its scenic value. Every effort to maintain these forests must be encouraged.

Door Peninsula residents have always had a deep appreciation for their trees and a strong desire to preserve them. Amid the forests of Glidden Drive, North Bay, Marshall's Point and the Black Ash Swamp are found maple, beech, basswood, birch, white pine, cedar and tamarack. And somewhere in those forests the heart of the peninsula is found as well, anchored in the soil and turning sunlight into life.

The grand vistas for which Door County is noted add a distinct aura to the peninsula. Viewed from the surrounding water these undeveloped bluffs provide a wonderful buffer of green space from developed areas nearby.

Today, however, escarpment forests are threatened. Development has already begun on the three-mile-

long Egg Harbor escarpment. At the tip of the peninsula, Death's Door Bluff remains an important geographic landmark and prime habitat for rare cliff-dwelling plants. The bluff summit is covered by second-growth beech-maple while its terraced, moist cliffs are forested with white cedars. On Washington

The seas are calm at Cave Point County Park.

205

Island, Boyers Bluff towers above Lake Michigan. Its shaded cliffs and 200-acre upland forest remain rich in plant diversity.

Door Peninsula beaches have always attracted attention, whether as camping spots for the Indians who preceded white settlers or as landing sites for the logging ships that followed. Today, pressure is greater than ever to permanently alter the shoreline. Fish spawning sites are threatened by marinas. Shoreline forests are threatened by development and beaches are threatened by pollution.

But Door County has fared better than many other shoreside areas. Its landowners, visitors and leaders increasingly realize the value of a secluded beach and the importance of a forested sand dune. Today, attempts to develop pristine shoreline, especially the dunes and swales along Sturgeon Bay's shipping canal, must be met with the most effective tools at hand. Altering a beach or clearing a shoreside forest will forever mar the very attraction that makes this peninsula so appealing.

While opinions vary as to what should be done to preserve the peninsula's natural beauty, there is much common ground. Shopkeepers, developers and conservationists agree—the Door Peninsula is a unique natural wonder.

To stave off the rapid development of farms, fields, woodlands and wetlands on the peninsula, a group of Door County landowners banded together in 1986 to form Door County Land Trustees, Inc. The goal of this nonprofit organization is to "preserve open space, and to protect the unique character and traditional way of life on the peninsula." Convinced that state and local land-use controls alone can not stem the tide of development, this local organization advocates private initiative in the form of land conservation easements.

Filed at the courthouse, these easements take the form of permanent deed restrictions binding both the present and the future owners of the property to limiting development or encouraging continued agricultural use. It does not change ownership of the land, and the property can still be sold or left to heirs.

Baileys Harbor farm owner Ruth Neuman became the first Door County resident to set aside some 120 acres of her meadowland under a conservation easement. Her action assures this land will remain in its natural state in perpetuity. In filing the easement, Neuman said, "After I am gone, my restrictions live on. I do have the pleasant thought that the yellow lady slipper, the red fox, and the visiting cranes . . . will stay around." For more information regarding this grass-roots approach to land conservation contact: Door County Land Trustees, Inc., Box 345, Ephraim.

Another group on the front line of peninsula environmental action is the Door County Environmental Council. This Fish Creek–based group acts as the watchdog of the peninsula, and its inexpensive dues and informative newsletter will keep you abreast of upcoming issues. For more information contact: Door County Environmental Council, Fish Creek, WI 54212.

Those who love Door County find that the forests, beaches, bluffs and wetlands serve to sooth and inspire. To us, the loss of any of these diverse resources alter not only the landscape but also our lives.

No place can remain the same forever. Change adds vitality to this rugged peninsula. It creates jobs and adds to the quality of life. But it is clear there must be planned, orderly land management. What is wild must remain wild. What is indigenous must be allowed to thrive. What is pristine must not be destroyed. The future of Door County depends on us.

Po-Sho,

Craig Charles

PO-SHO
Potawatomi Indian word meaning goodbye.

AT A GLANCE

Door County

Population: 26,122
County Seat: Sturgeon Bay
Area: 491 Square Miles
Chamber of Commerce: Visit: Highway 57 at the entrance to
                            Sturgeon Bay
                            Write: Box 346, Sturgeon Bay, WI 54235
                            Phone: 414-743-4456
                            Office Hours: Mon–Fri, 8:00–5:00 P.M.
                            June through August, Sat, 10:00–4:00 P.M.

Emergency Numbers: Ambulance: No. Door: 868-3237
                                       So. Door: 743-2244
CRITICAL SITUATION   Hospital: 414-743-5566
DIAL 911   Sheriff: 414-743-2244

Fishing Hot Line (24-hr)   Phone: 414-743-7046
Snow Condition Hotline   Phone: 414-743-7046

State Parks/Trails

Peninsula State Park
Box 218
Fish Creek, WI 54212
414-868-3258

Newport State Park
475 S. Newport Lane
Ellison Bay, WI 54210
414-854-2500
*Backpack sites only

Whitefish Dunes State Park
Sturgeon Bay, WI 54235
414-823-2400
*Camping not available

Potawatomi State Park
3740 Park Drive
Sturgeon Bay, WI 54235
414-743-8869

Rock Island State Park
Washington Island, WI 54246
414-847-2235
*Access by boat only

Ahnapee State Trail
Sturgeon Bay, WI 54235
414-743-5123

Weather

| | | | | | AVERAGE TEMPERATURES | | | | | | | |
	JAN	FEB	MAR	APR	MAY	JUN	JUL	AUG	SEP	OCT	NOV	DEC
Green Bay	17	18	33	48	59	64	72	65	59	48	28	25
Sturgeon Bay	18	19	32	46	57	62	70	65	60	49	32	26
Washington Island	19	18	29	44	55	58	67	64	58	48	33	27

| | TEMPERATURES | PRECIPITATION | | |
	Record High/Low	Mean Rain (inches)	Mean Snow	Days With Rain
Sturgeon Bay	105/−29	27.2	40.3	63
Green Bay	104/−27	26.6	39.8	117

WEATHER INFORMATION:
Green Bay: 414-494-2363
Sturgeon Bay: 414-743-6577

ROAD CONSTRUCTION INFORMATION:
Statewide: 414-342-2211

Lighthouses

Sherwood Point	Sturgeon Bay
Potawatomi	Rock Island
Cana Island	Baileys Harbor
Sturgeon Bay Canal	Sturgeon Bay
Eagle	Peninsula State Park
Plum Island	Plum Island
Ridges Range Lights	Baileys Harbor
Chambers Island	Pilot Island

Inland Lakes

25 total but only six with adequate public access:

Kangaroo Lake	Mud Lake
Clark Lake	Little Lake
Europe Lake	Forestville Flowage (Lake Ahnapee)

Golf Courses

Lost Creek (414-743-6880)   Sturgeon Bay
Pepperdine (414-743-7246)   Sturgeon Bay
Peninsula (414-854-9921)   Peninsula State Park
Maxwelton Braes (414-839-2321)   Baileys Harbor
Alpine (414-868-3232)   Egg Harbor
Bay Ridge (414-854-4085)   Sister Bay
Maple Grove (414-847-2017)   Washington Island

Public Tennis Courts*

Otumba Park   Sturgeon Bay
Sunset Park   Sturgeon Bay
Fish Creek Village Park   Fish Creek
Ephraim Village Playground   Ephraim
Sister Bay Village Park   Sister Bay
Island Camping & Recreation   Washington Island
Ellison Bay Town Park   Ellison Bay
Jacksonport Village Park, County V Jacksonport

*Fees required at most tennis courts.

Door County Public Water Access

The abundance of water is one of the primary attractions of Door County. Accordingly, efforts have been made to make water frontage available to the public.

Today, over ninety water access areas have been established along Green Bay, Lake Michigan and inland lakes on the peninsula. The amount of water frontage at the various access sites ranges from several miles at state parks like Peninsula, Whitefish Dunes and Newport to less than 100 feet, as often occurs at road endings.

Of the 92 access areas, 53 are not associated with public park land. Rather, they are usually road endings and/or hiking trails that have been dedicated to the public as part of state platting requirements. Most of these sites are unimproved, but they do afford room to stretch out a beach blanket or slide in a canoe. The map provided will assist you in utilizing these unmarked public access sites.

Unfortunately, not all of these access sites always appear open to the public. Sometimes, adjacent property owners discourage folks from using these sites. Don't be intimidated. Just be sure you remain on the stretch of beach within the public domain.

PUBLIC WATER ACCESSES
not associated with parks and recreation areas

SUNRISE RD.

BALSAM DR.

SUNSET LN.

HARBOR RD.

GARRET BAY

HWY. 42 (NORTHPORT)

EUROPE LAKE RD.

WATERS END RD.

BAY RD.

APPLEPORT RD.

COTTAGE ROW RD.

PENINSULA PLAYERS RD.

JUDDVILLE RD.

WHITE CLIFF LN.

DOCK RD.

SUNSET LN.

CANA ISLAND RD.

RIDGES DR.

EAST LAKE LN.

MCARDLE LN.

KANGAROO BEACH RD.

O'BRIEN RD.

SUNSET LN.

LADY SLIPPER POND

JORNS RD.

SCHAUER LN.

TOWN LINE RD.

CLARKS LAKE RD.

WHITEFISH BAY

SHERWOOD POINT RD.

ELIASON RD.

SAND BAY POINT LN.

SANDY POINT RD.

SAND BAY LN.

RILEYS BAY RD.

GOLDEN ROD LN.

ARROWHEAD LN.

BITTERSWEET LN.

HEMLOCK LN.

DEERPATH LN.

LILLY BAY

CTY. HWY. TT

KICKAPOO DR.

CHIPPEWA DR.

WINNEBAGO DR.

CHEROKEE DR.

CROWFOOT DR.

MENOMONIE DR.

CTY. HWY. N

ELMS RD.

SOLONA RD.

OAKWOOD RD.

CEDAR RD.

SCHUYLER RD.

211

Islands at a Glance

Washington Island: Over 500 year-round residents live on Washington Island, the largest and oldest Icelandic community outside of Iceland. Settled by fishermen, commerical fishing tugs still chug out of beautiful Jackson Harbor in search of white-fish. A 40-minute ferry ride from Northport.

Detroit Island: A privately held island that guards the entrance to Washington Island's Detroit Harbor.

Plum Island: A U.S. Coast Guard station on Plum Island continues to watch over Death's Door Passage. The remainder of the island is leased to the state of Wisconsin and would become part of Grand Traverse Islands State Park if this proposal ever receives the support it deserves.

Rock Island: Rock Island State Park lies off the northeast corner of Washington Island. Sand beach. A ten-minute ferry ride from Jackson Harbor on Washington Island.

Chambers Island: About five miles from the mainland at Fish Creek, Chamber's Island has an island on a lake on the island. Or is that a lake on the island on the lake? A Catholic retreat house here provides solitude and contemplation to ponder such questions.

Horseshoe Island: Two miles off the Peninsula State Park shore. Horseshoe Island provides refuge for boaters and a pleasant picnic site for paddlers. Administered as part of Peninsula State Park.

Sister Islands: A pair of state owned twins that gave the village of Sister Bay its name.

Hat Island: Playgoers enjoy watching the sunset behind Hat Island while nursing a frosty beer before performances at the Peninsula Players Theatre in a Garden. Seagulls and terns appreciate the nesting opportunities presented by this privately owned island.

The Strawberry Islands: Adventure, Jack, Pirate and Little Strawberry make up this short chain of privately owned islands. These islands are visible from the tower at Peninsula State Park.

Pilot Island: Wave at the seagulls from the Washington Island Ferry as you pass Pilot Island off the tip of Detroit Island. So named because it was used by early sailors navigating the Death's Door Passage.

Hog Island: Hog Island is a National Wildlife Refuge off the eastern shores of Washington Island. You'll find seagulls and terns here raising their young.

Spider and Gravel Islands: Located east of Newport State Park, these wildlife refuges provide nesting opportunities for shorebirds and resting opportunities for their migrating feathered friends.

Cana Island: This nine-acre island is connected by causeway to the mainland. Home to an historic lighthouse that was once oil operated, but today automated. Usually you can reach this federally owned island without getting your feet wet.

Photo Credits

George R. Cassidy/Third Coast, 12, 105
Craig Charles, 8, 21, 40, 51, 126, 156, 186, 190
David L. Denemark/Third Coast, 81
Ken Dequaine, 56, 110, 112, 138, 176, 180, 184
Sue Hagen/Third Coast, 164
Christine Linder, 63
William Meyer/Third Coast, 72
Brent Nicastro, 67, 95
Todd V. Phillips/Third Coast, 88, 121, 199, 202
Beth Quade, 102
Willard Romantini, 161
J.P. Slater/Third Coast, 197
John Touscany/Third Coast, 26
Mark Wallner, 33
Ken Wardius/Third Coast, 145
Wisconsin Department of Tourism Development, x,
    46, 92, 129, 132, 150, 169, 205

Front Cover Photo of Cave Point County Park by Ken
    Dequaine
Front Cover Inset Photo of Julie and Craig Charles by
    Craig Charles
Back Cover Photo of Europe Lake by Craig Charles

Map Art by Donna Frankenberg

Also from NORTHWORD
PRESS, INC

ABOUT COWS
Sara Rath

About Cows is an affectionately humorous tribute to the domestic animal which produces 20% of the agricultural wealth of this country. Anyone with any connections with cows will love this illustrated collection of cow history, trivia and nostalgia. Sprinkled with anecdotes from farmers, cheesemakers, veterinarians and others who have crossed paths with cows.

    About Cows features 32 color photographs of cows in their natural habitat and dozens of fascinating black-and-white illustrations.

$14.95 • 9¼ × 7⅜, 256 pages, paper • ISBN 0-942802-75-6

PRAIRIE VISIONS
Robert Gard

Author of thirty-eight books, Robert Gard is the premier storyteller of The Heartlands. *Prairie Visions* is his autobiographical journey into the heart of America. The book distills the stories and legends of mid-America and masterfully captures the mystique of the Heartland and its people.

    Prairie Visions traces the steps of this award-winning author from his boyhood home in depression-racked Kansas to New York where he developed a regional theater program and to Wisconsin where his literary talents took firm root. Besides providing an intriguing record of the places he has been and the people he has met, *Prairie Visions* presents a spiritual profile of the Heartland itself.

$14.95 • 6½ × 9½, 320 pages, cloth • ISBN 0-942802-54-3

GUIDE TO WISCONSIN OUTDOORS
Jim Umhoefer

An all-new edition of this popular guide. Expanded and updated, it covers not only more than 70 Wisconsin State Parks, Forests and Trails, but also all of the National Parks, Forests and Wildlife Refuges. Included are a detailed description of the extensive Ice Age National Scenic Reserve and the Ice Age National Scenic Trail, exciting photographs and beautifully drawn maps. The guide is useful, informative, fun to read and suited to all seasons. Hikers, campers, picnickers, vacationers and anyone wanting to be outside in Wisconsin will find this guide invaluable.

$19.95 • 6 × 9, 468 pages, paper • ISBN 1-55971-009-8

OLD PENINSULA DAYS

The definitive history of Door County, a vacation paradise which attracts over 2 million visitors annually. More than local history, Holand, in his beautifully written narrative, details the step-by-step creation of a unique American community. The region is rich with cultural heritage, starting with the first missionary exploration only 14 years after the Pilgrims landed at Plymouth Rock.

$9.95 • 6 × 9, 256 pages, paper • ISBN 1-55971-057-8

FIRE & ICE
Don Davenport and Robert W. Wells

Combines two deadly disaster epics under one cover. "These are shocking tales of nature's fury: the 1958 killer storm that sent the big ore carrier *Carl D. Bradley* bubbling to the bottom of Lake Michigan, and the 1871 holocaust that charred bodies and blackened the landscape in Peshtigo, Wisconsin, the most disastrous fire in American history.

    "*Shipwreck on Lake Michigan*, by Don Davenport, a Great Lakes scholar, is the kind of story a reader can't put down. Robert Wells tells the searing story of *Fire at Peshtigo* with the sure hand of a veteran newspaperman."—*The Milwaukee Journal*

$13.95 • 5½ × 8½, 450 pages, paper • ISBN 0-942802-04-7

OLD WORLD WISCONSIN

First published in 1944, this delightful book explores haunts, hilltops and byways and the ethnic traditions of Old World homes and families. Even more valuable today in the light of cultural assimilation, these vanishing epochs remain alive and vibrant through the author's deft touch. Told in a style that makes this new edition valuable, both as reliable history and as vivid literature.

$9.95 • 6 × 9, 256 pages, paper • ISBN 1-55971-056-X

To receive our free color catalog or order any of these books call toll free 1-800-336-5666. NorthWord Press Inc., Box 1360, Minocqua, WI 54548.